Can God Be Trusted?

Can God Be Trusted?

Faith and the Challenge of Evil

John G. Stackhouse, Jr.

OXFORD
UNIVERSITY PRESS

OXFORD
UNIVERSITY PRESS

Oxford   New York
Athens   Auckland   Bangkok   Bogotá   Buenos Aires
Calcutta   Cape Town   Chennai   Dar es Salaam   Delhi
Florence   Hong Kong   Istanbul   Karachi   Kuala Lumpur
Madrid   Melbourne   Mexico City   Mumbai   Nairobi   Paris
São Paulo   Singapore   Taipei   Tokyo   Toronto   Warsaw

and associated companies in
Berlin   Ibadan

Copyright © 1998 by John G. Stackhouse, Jr.

First published in 1998 by Oxford University Press, Inc.
198 Madison Avenue, New York, New York 10016

First issued as an Oxford University Press paperback, 2000

Oxford is a registered trademark of Oxford University Press

Library of Congress Cataloging-in-Publication Data
Stackhouse, John Gordon
Can God be trusted? : faith and the challenge of evil/
John G. Stackhouse, Jr.
p. cm. Includes bibliographical references and index.
ISBN 0-19-511727-1 (cloth)
ISBN 0-19-513791-4 (pbk.)
1. Theodicy. 2. Good and evil. 3. Trust in God—Christianity.
I. Title.
BT160.S82   1998
231'.8—dc21   97-50588
The author gratefully acknowledges permission to reprint
several selections from Fyodor Dostoyevsky, *The Brothers Karamazov*,
trans. David McDuff, © 1993.

1 3 5 7 9 8 6 4 2
Printed in the United States of America
on acid-free paper

to Mom and Dad

CONTENTS

ACKNOWLEDGMENTS

WRITING THIS BOOK WAS MADE EASIER because of grants received from the Social Sciences and Humanities Research Council of Canada and because of a research leave granted for the academic year 1995–96 by the University of Manitoba.

The resulting book is better than it would have been because of the help of a number of generous people. Jon Pott of the Wm. B. Eerdmans Publishing Company and Rodney Clapp of InterVarsity Press furnished me with several pertinent books from their worthy lines. William Hasker kindly sent me several of his excellent articles on related subjects. Michael Peterson's fine anthology on the problem of evil, cited in the notes, introduced me to key texts early in my research. Alvin Plantinga tutored me patiently in the finer points of his philosophy, although I may yet not have gotten it quite right. Mark Fretz, David Frum, and Philip Yancey graciously offered advice to this ivory-tower scholar on the world of trade publishing. And my research assistants Rachel Van Caeseele and Patricia Loewen were models of cheerful industry and high competence.

Audiences of lectures I have given on this subject at the University of Manitoba and at Regent College, Vancouver, provoked me by their questions to revise my thought in several places. The following readers each offered wise advice on earlier versions of the manuscript: Bruce Annan, Rob Boschmann, Matt Floding, Larry Hurtado, Klaus Klostermaier, Marie Loewen, Valerie Lunau, Anne McKenzie, Chris Manuel, Martin Marty, Mickey Maudlin, Charlie Newsom, Joni Nicolou, Sheila Parks, Clark Pinnock, Michael Stack, Brent Stackhouse, and Cindra Stackhouse Taetzsch. These readers must be excused from any responsibility for what I have done with their good counsel, of course, especially since some of them continue to disagree with what I have written herein.

Special assistance was rendered by Gerald McDermott, Cornelius Plantinga, and Nicholas Wolterstorff, who not only offered incisive and thorough critiques of the manuscript, but then nonetheless recommended it to Oxford University Press. Cynthia Read, executive editor at that press, early on championed the book, warts and all, and performed much-needed and much-appreciated surgery on those warts. Those that remain must be attributed to my stubbornness, not to her lack of skill.

My wife, Kari, and my sons, Trevor, Joshua, and Devon, are four of my favorite reasons to thank God in spite of evil, and they helped with this book immeasurably just by being my family.

My parents, Yvonne and John Stackhouse, taught me by word and example that God can be trusted, and to them I gratefully dedicate this book.

Can God Be Trusted?

INTRODUCTION

Here is tonight's newscast:

"There was more trouble today in the Middle East. Three terrorists commandeered a school bus in east Jerusalem and then set off explosives that killed both themselves and . . .

"A major storm hit the west coast of India last night. Red Cross officials in Bombay estimate that dozens of people were killed, more than 300 injured, and thousands left homeless by the cyclone. Waves over forty feet high crashed ashore at . . .

"It is day four of the siege of the presidential palace mounted by military rebels in the African capital of . . .

"The White House announced this morning that yet another welfare program will be discontinued. This is the third such cutback this month, and administration spokesperson Maria Estevez said that Congress was to blame because . . .

"Here in the city, the trial of former mayor Stu Gardiner began this afternoon. Gardiner has been indicted on three counts of election fraud and has been linked to organized crime in his efforts to bring legalized gambling to . . .

"A four-car pileup on Route 261 last night resulted in five deaths, with three more victims listed as critical in Northwest General Hospital. The driver of a late-model pickup truck that jumped the median and crashed into oncoming traffic has been arrested on drunk driving charges . . .

"Efforts continue to find a bone marrow donor for little Monica Pedrowski. The six-year-old has been diagnosed with a rare form of cancer, and none of the members of her family is a proper match for the procedure which could save her life. Officials at Grace Memorial Hospital are appealing to . . .

"And that's the news. Good night."

Our televisions, radios, newspapers, and magazines pour out a never-ending stream of tragedy, disaster, selfishness, and absurdity. Our eyes glaze over, and our hearts grow numb with compassion fatigue. But every once in a while a story grips us, we sit up straight, and the old questions return: "How could this happen? What kind of a world is this?" And we might ask one of the oldest questions of all, "How could a good and almighty God possibly allow such evil to occur?"

People who are in the midst of grief or catastrophe or peril probably will find some of this book to be too abstract for them, too coolly distant from their immediate pain. What these people need instead is comfort, and especially the comfort of those who can truly sympathize. The heartfelt reflections of other suffering persons can be helpful, and I refer to some of these in the notes.[1]

I offer this book instead to those who want to consider seriously the question of faith in God *before* crushing evil befalls them or someone they care about. I offer it to people who want to prepare themselves to face the reality of life, which includes the reality of evil, with as many intellectual tools in the cupboard as they can get. I offer it to those who are so offended by God's apparent mismanagement of the world that they cannot take faith in God seriously. And I offer it also to people who have experienced bitter trouble and who long for a helpful, hopeful word on the subject of faith in God.

There are three kinds of books that respond to questions about God and evil. One kind is technical: philosophy or theology that deals with God and evil as abstractions in order to arrive at the greatest possible conceptual clarity. This kind of book is important because the intellectual issues it discusses are important—among the most basic questions human beings ever ask. But for most of us, the wisdom of such arguments remains remote in the seminar rooms of academe.

Another kind of book is pastoral: practical advice on how to endure suffering, or how to care for others who suffer. This kind of book is important because we all need to know what to do to cope as best we can with the evil we encounter. But such books can fail to offer us some of the help we need if they stick only to what we should do, and don't help us to think clearly about the whys and wherefores behind the disappointments and disasters we face.

This book fits between the other two kinds. It gathers up the fruits of front-rank philosophy and theology and offers them to nonspecialists, to thoughtful people who want to be able to think more clearly about these matters so that they may respond to evil more adequately when they face it. We need more than good ideas, of course, to respond adequately to the challenges of life. But what we do to respond to life's challenges depends in large part upon what we think about reality—about what evil actually is, for instance, or about whether there is a God and what sort of deity God might be. This book offers ideas that, I hope, will clear away some unnecessary confusions that arise from our encounter with evil. It then goes beyond such brush clearing to establish some foundations for faith, to provide some reasonable bases upon which an informed person can trust God in spite of evil.

Some dimensions of the question of God and evil remain, I believe, intractable mysteries. It may even be true (I think it is) that some things that we think we want to know will *always* remain unknown to us, whether because in the nature of the case it is impossible for us to comprehend them, or because in God's kind wisdom they are kept from us. What we can properly do, however, is to inquire as far as we are able. We can seek knowledge where it may be found. And then we can consider whether we have adequate grounds for holding on to our belief in God, if we believe, or for entertaining such belief if we do not.

Such grounds do not substitute for faith, but they can form a good part of its basis. Faith by its nature requires at least some knowledge. There is no such thing as "blind faith." No one believes *anything* for no reason at all. We get our beliefs from somewhere, even if we cannot say where, how, or why. We might observe how insulting to blind people the phrase "blind faith" is, and how false as well. It is obvious that the visually impaired nonetheless sense the world in many other ways. Similarly, I suggest, people whose convictions do not arise from philo-sophical reasoning or sense experience may yet have every right to be judged as rationally respectable because those beliefs might have been gained through some other valid avenue of knowledge.

Children believe in gravity, for example, without any theorizing about the relations of masses in space, but I doubt that any of us would say that children believe in gravity without cause. Similarly, some of us may grow up believing in God because of the homes we live in, or because of spiritual experiences we enjoyed even very young, and not because we became convinced of God's existence through abstract argument. Yet we are justified to trust the testimony of religious parents and friends as we grow up, or the validity of reli-gious experiences we have had, at least until we encounter sufficient reason not to do so.

Furthermore, however we acquire particular beliefs (this is quite a vexed question in contemporary philosophy), most people hang on to only those beliefs that seem to work in their ongoing life experi-ence, those beliefs that they have "good reason" of some sort to main-tain. Complete closed-mindedness-once-convinced is what some-times is meant by "blind faith," but again, blind faith is rare, if not impossible. Few of us remain utterly impervious to countervailing evidence just because we once made up our minds about something.

In sum, even if we cannot set out comprehensively just why we believe this or that (and to do so might tax the ability of even a skilled philosopher), we all have reasons for why we believe.[2] Now, we may disagree with each other as to whether we have *adequate* grounds for believing this or that. But we all have *some* grounds. Faith—and I mean just everyday, ordinary "faith" here, not necessarily anything specifically religious—is going beyond what one knows, yes. But it is *based* upon what one knows. Audrey assesses rationally, if not necessarily consciously, whether she can put her faith in this chair as she sits, or in this boat as she pushes off from the dock. In a similar way, Joshua weighs up reasons for and against trusting a *person* with confidential information, or partnership in a business, or sharing life in marriage, or baby-sitting his children.

This is the way, I suggest, to consider the issue of religious faith as well. No religion that I know of demands that its devotees just believe for no reason at all, nor does any ask for faith to the exclusion of rational inquiry. Instead, each religion is confident that it explains reality better than does any other, and helps us respond to reality better than does any other, and thus is worthy of commitment. So the various religions themselves encourage us to ask what many reasonable people ask anyway: whether we have adequate reasons to put our trust in God. This book poses just this question in terms of one of the most powerful challenges to faith, the reality of evil. Can we believe in God in spite of evil?

Part One begins with the most basic question of all: whether there is a problem here in the first place. If we consider other religions and philosophies, we find that the problem of God and evil, as many of us understand it, simply disappears if we define "God" or "evil" in a different way. Subscribing to one of these alternatives, to be sure, might present new problems. C. S. Lewis, when faced with bitter grief, was deeply afraid not that he would stop believing in God, but that his beliefs about God would change in a dismaying direction:

> The real danger is coming to believe such dreadful things about Him. The conclusion I dread is not, "So there's no God after all," but, "So this is what God's really like. Deceive yourself no longer."[3]

We must face squarely the prospect that other religions and philosophies proffer answers to our question, but they do so by changing its terms: a different kind of God or gods, or a different understanding of the nature—or even the reality—of evil.

If we proceed instead with the question of God and evil in classical terms, that of an all-good and all-powerful God who nonetheless allows evil in the cosmos, then we must go on to stare steadily at evil in all of its variety and depth, without dodging any hard cases. Part One does this, and then concludes the posing of the problem by recognizing several other problems—such as the problem of good ("If there is evil, there must be good, so where does it come from?") and the problem of meaning ("Is there any ultimate sense that can be made of things, and therefore some sense that can be made of evil?")—that are so closely related to the central question of God and evil that they, too, deserve attention in this discussion.

The purpose of Part One, therefore, is to set the agenda as fully and clearly as possible, and Part Two responds to the questions thus posed. It begins by considering ways of reframing the issues. Must everything work out properly in this world, or is there an afterlife which we ought to take into account? Is suffering simply an evil to be avoided, or can it sometimes be a means to good ends? And are we human beings somehow implicated in matters that we perhaps would like to think are entirely God's fault?

The book then steers toward considering the ultimate meaning of life, especially as it pertains to the question of God and evil. Perhaps if the point of human existence is not primarily to avoid unhappiness, but to gain some other, greater good, then the presence of suffering and evil in our world can be seen in a new and hopeful way. The philosophical Free Will Defense is a particular Christian view of the matter, and this defense is then extended here to a possible explanation of why the world is as it is: a world that actually meets our needs and does us good after all.

At this point, however, my argument asserts that no comprehensive answer is available to us. The search for an explanation for any and all evil is doomed to frustration. Yet the book's longest chapter then goes on to take a different tack, one that nonetheless can satisfy our inquiry. It offers a multidimensional case for believing in God in spite of evil. We cannot know the answer to *why* God runs the world as God does, but we *can* know *whether* God can be trusted to do so in a way that is good.

What I offer, then, is this: a description of what we're up against in our struggle against evil, and good reasons to believe in God even in the throes of that struggle. In short, I want to offer hope that, despite appearances and agonies, we really can trust God in spite of evil.

PART ONE

Problems

CHAPTER ONE

Is There a Problem?

Is God willing to prevent evil, but not able?
then he is impotent. Is he able, but not
willing? then is he malevolent. Is he both able
and willing? whence then is evil?

David Hume,
Dialogues concerning Natural Religion, 1779

SCOTTISH PHILOSOPHER DAVID HUME, echoing the Greek philosopher Epicurus, thus states the so-called problem of evil in classic skeptical form. But an ancient Hebrew poet screams out the problem of evil as many *believers* feel it:

My God, my God, why have you forsaken me? Why are you so far from helping me, from the words of my groaning? O my God, I cry by day, but you do not answer; and by night, but find no rest. (Psalm 22:1, 2 NRSV)

Many of us lack Hume's concision and the Psalmist's eloquence, but we feel the same way when evil confronts us. How can God be all-powerful and all-good, and yet evil afflict us so widely and deeply?[1]

Most of this book responds directly to Hume's central challenge. Let us pause, however, to consider some implications in his litany of questions. Hume wondered whether God is not able to prevent evil, or is malevolent and does not want to do so. He might also have wondered whether evil is real or, if it is, whether it is something for which God ought to be held responsible. If we understand differently such crucial terms as "God" and "evil," then we no longer have the problem of evil as Hume (along with most Jews, Christians, and Muslims) understood it.

Hume posed his challenge in early modern Europe, a culture in which almost everyone could be assumed to have a basic faith in a supreme God as revealed in the Jewish and Christian Scriptures, and to share a basic understanding of the nature of evil. Those cultural assumptions do not hold in Europe or North America today, and especially not elsewhere in the world. Other religions and philosophies have such different views of God or the gods, of evil, and of the relationship between the divine and the world, that this particular "problem of evil" disappears.[2] These alternatives, that is, "solve" the theistic problem of evil by redefinition.

WHAT IS GOD?

Monotheists, or *theists* for short, believe in one God. In Judaism, Christianity, and Islam, this one God traditionally is understood to be all-powerful (*omnipotent*). Now, occasionally a Sunday-school teacher has been afflicted with clever questions such as, "Can God create a load so big that God cannot lift it?" Such questions, though, amount to logical contradictions, and traditional theism has never affirmed that God is capable of performing such things. Instead, theism affirms that God is able to do anything God wants to do. God cannot perform a logical contradiction because it is, strictly speaking, nothing at all, like a square circle. Nor can God do anything that would be contrary to God's moral nature, because this would be a *moral* contradiction. This would be like God being completely committed to truth and then also lying on occasion—the idea just doesn't make sense. It is in this qualified sense, therefore, that God is omnipotent.

As a kind of extension of God's power, God's knowledge is also absolute (a quality termed *omniscience*). Theists traditionally affirm that since God is spirit and universally present, God knows all of the present, all of the past, and all of the future. God's knowledge of the future (from our point of view in the present, this looks like *foreknowledge*) is variously explained by theologians and philosophers. Some, borrowing from the Platonic tradition, believe that God is somehow beyond time itself, or at least our timeline, and looks on the unfolding of the world perhaps as an author looks on a novel she has written. For the characters in the story, the plot moves forward in time, but for the author who can flip back and forth at will and who sits outside the book's timeline entirely, the plot is already completed. Perhaps, others have conjectured, God indwells all of time simultaneously just as God indwells all of space. Still others believe that because God has a comprehensive knowledge of everything in the universe, God can see what will happen in the future by extrapolating correctly from the present. However God's omniscience is understood, though, it is a cardinal quality that all traditional theists assert.

For our purposes, then, let us include omniscience as a category of God's omnipotence. Then we turn to the other quality of God's being that is crucial to this discussion, God's absolute goodness (sometimes termed *omnibenevolence*). However mysterious God's work in the world appears to be—indeed, however contradictory and even *evil* God's work in the world appears to be—theists affirm that God is always and only good. Sometimes it is obvious that God is good; sometimes it is not. But everything God thinks and wills and does is good. In fact, our own understanding of what is good properly derives from God's revealing to us, through word and deed, what is good.

Theism does not affirm that God is always "nice" or pleasant or kindly. God's goodness is absolute purity, as much like the purity of a blast furnace (the Christian Bible calls God "a consuming fire") as it is like the indulgence of a sweet grandmother. God always does the right thing; God always wills what is best; God always thinks without error, incompleteness, or prejudice. Such a God may not always be likable, nor always comfortable. But such a God may well be worthy of worship.

In the moral realm, when theists declare that God is good, they mean a God who thinks and wills and acts with goodness, and thus a God who is personal. To be sure, the full nature of God's personality is beyond our understanding. This truth has led some theologians to suggest that God is "beyond" personality.[3] Such abstractions, however, regrettably end up portraying God as *less* than personal, as a vague kind of force or energy or universal law. For traditional theism, however, God is a richer, more complex, more wonderful personality than we are.

This is why Judaism, Christianity, and Islam habitually use personal pronouns for God. Now each of those religions developed within, and to a considerable extent reinforced, the patriarchal structure of each culture. In such cultures, God revealed Godself primarily (although not exclusively) in masculine roles of authority, initiative, and caregiving vis-à-vis God's creation and, particularly, in relation to God's people. Thus God appears as king, master, father, husband, and so on. Given these dominant metaphors, masculine pronouns most commonly are used in Jewish, Christian, and Muslim theology, as well as in the Scriptures themselves.

This matter must not be left here, however. For traditional theism also affirms that God is not essentially male: God is spirit, and beyond sex. Furthermore, God created human beings as male and female and both in God's own image. And only in the conjunction of male and female, masculine and feminine, is there the intended human representation of God. Thus it is well for us to keep in mind the feminine aspect of the divine as we consider such a basic question as how God administers the world.[4]

Now, if God were good only in the sense that God is not evil, that God is just, that everything God thinks and feels and says and does is right, then we would not yet have the God of Judaism or Christianity or Islam. For these classic monotheisms affirm at least one more basic proposition about God: God is love. Fundamental, that is, to God's nature and activity is benevolence of this sort as well: not merely moral purity, but a passionate and active care for God's creatures. (For example, all but one section, or *sura*, of the Qur'ān begins with this phrase: "In the name of Allāh, the Compassionate, the Merciful.") So the goodness of God includes both God's moral rectitude (or "righteousness") and God's deep concern for, and exertion on behalf of, the creatures God loves.

Thus theism believes that there is one God, creator and sustainer of the universe, directing history with omnipotence toward a goal of final goodness according to God's own omnibenevolence. So why is there evil?

GOD COULD BE OTHERWISE

Perhaps God is not all-powerful. Many religions in the world have understood there to be no single, supreme, omnipotent being, but rather a number of gods (thus *polytheism*), each with his, or her, or its own power and limitation. Whether the gods of the Aztecs of Central America, the tribal divinities of Australian aborigines, or the deities of ancient Egypt, Greece, and Rome, these gods are variously greater and lesser, more and less splendid and influential, and not even the monarch of the gods is all-powerful.

Occasionally, a religion asserts the existence of two supreme deities. Usually one is identified with good and the other with evil. Zoroastrianism, the religion of ancient Persia and still a living religion today, has espoused this *dualism* at certain times in its historical development. So have forms of Gnostic religion (from the Greek word for the secret knowledge taught by these cults, *gnōsis*) that arose in the later Roman Empire and have shown up here and there in Western culture ever since. The two great gods are locked in a cosmic struggle, neither one prevailing everywhere and always. Most forms of dualism, however, teach that eventually the good god will triumph.

In the traditional monotheistic religions themselves, furthermore, some theologians have suggested that God is not all-powerful. In our own day, one of the most popular books on the subject of God and evil (*When Bad Things Happen to Good People*) was written by a rabbi who, in the face of family tragedy, felt compelled to conclude that God was indeed all-good, but not all-powerful. In this view, God always means well, but simply cannot make things come out right: some crucial matters remain beyond God's control.

Surely one can allow that each of these options makes considerable sense of the topsy-turvy nature of the world as we experience it. For our world does not seem to present a single, uniform goodness under the guidance of a good God, but rather a distressing mixture of good and evil with no one apparently in final control.

Other thoughtful people have concluded that the evil in the world is best explained by tracing evil to the very heart of things—to the character of the gods themselves. The Greek gods on Mount Olympus, for example, are a mischievous bunch. They are forever plotting against each other and each other's devotees when they aren't embroiled in open conflict. The whole Trojan War is a contest of the gods more than it is of the Greeks and the Trojans, as each god helps his or her favorite warrior against the champions of his or her enemies. Even Zeus, chief of the gods, is no paragon of moral virtue. Zeus spends most of his time jealously preserving his lordly prerogatives against the other deities with diplomacy, trickery, or sheer strength. And when he isn't doing that, he is sneaking off Mount Olympus to seduce or, if necessary, to rape some comely mortal woman. However incredible such stories may seem to us today, though, we might admit that to see the cosmos, and human society in particular, as subject to the whims of this capricious crowd of deities goes a long way toward explaining our unpredictable and dangerous world.

Half a world away, millions of Indians for hundreds of years have venerated Lord Śiva as supreme divinity. Sometimes Śiva is pictured as both male and female, but more commonly as a muscular male with a beautiful female consort, because of his mighty generative power. In the mainstream of the form of Hinduism that views Śiva as the supreme Lord (Śaivism), Śiva is the Creator of all. But he is also often depicted with two faces, one kindly and wise, the other dark and fierce. For Śiva is also the Destroyer. Indeed, his prototype in the ancient Indian religious texts, the Vedas, is Rudra "the Howler," god of thunderous storms. In some myths, Śiva generates the cosmos, cycles it through its maturation and decay, and brings it finally to a cataclysmic end—out of which, perhaps (depending on the myth), he may bring a new world into being. Thus when Indians have encountered a world that has seemed sometimes lush and sometimes desolate, sometimes rich and sometimes poor, sometimes creative and sometimes destructive, many of them have seen the work of Lord Śiva at the very core of things.

Perhaps, then, the divine is thoroughly good, but is not powerful enough to prevent all evil. Perhaps, instead, the divine is all-powerful, but is a mix of good and evil. A third option, though, would be that God is omnipotent, and not what one would call both good and evil, but instead remote and even, perhaps, essentially impersonal.

The Greek philosopher Aristotle believed in a God of sorts. But Aristotle's God was the so-called Unmoved Mover, the primary cause of the universe that set everything in motion but was itself uninfluenced by anything else that happened. During the Enlightenment in early modern Europe, a number of notable intellectuals adopted a similar understanding of God. God was a sort of divine clockmaker who built and wound up the universe, and then let it go its own way. This view is known as *deism*, and was held by Voltaire, Rousseau, Benjamin Franklin, and Thomas Jefferson.[5]

In tribal religions the world over, in Africa and Australia and the Americas, a somewhat similar deity shows up here and there. This is a Great Spirit or primal God who is responsible for the existence of everything else. At the beginning of time this God created at least the original stuff of the cosmos—however much that stuff has been affected by other beings since then. In some mythologies, this God continues to be the underlying ground or source of all that exists. But, say most of these myths (especially those that are unlikely to have been influenced by missionary stories about the Christian or Muslim Supreme Being), at some time in the remote past all human contact with this God was interrupted. Note that in such myths there is the conviction that in the earliest days there *was* substantial contact between creatures and this Supreme Being. Whether humans committed some offense against this God, or the God removed himself for his own reasons, or some other catastrophe broke the accord, it remains that since that time this God has had almost nothing to do with human beings. Thus in such tribal religions this Supreme God is not worshiped. The intermediate spirits that affect daily life are venerated instead.

In certain forms of Indian religion, notably in the form of Hinduism known as Advaita jñānamārga ("non-dualist way of knowledge"), the Supreme Reality is Brahman, the undivided unity of all that exists.

This ocean of being, into which individual beings (such as human souls) one day will enter like raindrops, is truly beyond personality. It is a kind of energy field, the original and final unity within and through which everything exists. Thus it makes no sense to speak of God having a moral nature, as being good or evil or both, for Ultimate Reality has no personality at all. As the student Svetaketu was told by his master in one of the great scriptures of this Hindu tradition:

> The rivers in the east flow eastward, the rivers in the west flow westward, and all enter into the sea. From sea to sea they pass, the clouds lifting them to the sky as vapor and sending them down as rain. And as these rivers, when they are united with the sea, do not know whether they are this or that river, likewise all those creatures that I have named, when they have come back from Brahman, know not whence they came.
>
> All those beings have their self in him alone. He is the truth. He is the subtle essence of all. He is the Self. And that, Svetaketu, *that art thou.*[6]

Thinkers around the globe have taken the next step and suggested that there is no Supreme Deity at all. Strands of the two dominant Chinese religions of Confucianism and Daoism, so different from each other, nonetheless together affirm this fundamental teaching. Confucianism arose during a time of intense and prolonged social upheaval in ancient China around 500 B.C.E. Kong-zi (the Latinized form of whose name is "Confucius") devised a philosophy of life that bound human beings together in a clear, comprehensive code of community. "A place for everything, and everything in its place" could well be a Confucian maxim, for this detailed order sets out correctness or "propriety" (li) for every member of society. If everyone pursues his or her place in this order, then each will grow toward full "humanness," or *ren,* treating each thing and each person in exact appropriateness to its nature and role. Thus will the whole society enjoy harmony—a chief virtue in traditional Chinese culture.

Confucianism is not merely an order of external rules, but an attitude toward life, toward fitting in with the Way (or *dao*) of things for the benefit of all. This attitude is focused upon this life, not upon some life to come. Traditional Chinese ancestor veneration and a variety of other spiritual concerns are maintained by Confucianists, especially at the popular level. But such pursuits round out what is at the highest level an essentially secular, this-worldly philosophy of balance and justice. Heaven (Tian) for Kong-zi is not the abode of some personal divinity, but a sort of impersonal divine ordering principle to which one owes reverence. Spiritual realities thus retreat into the background of a religion that is, fundamentally, atheistic. For as Kong-zi said, "Devote yourself to the proper demands of the people, respect the ghosts and spirits but keep them at a distance—this may be called wisdom."[7]

The religion of Daoism understands the Way (dao) quite differently. It rejects all external constraints and thus rejects the whole thrust of Confucianism. Instead, it celebrates the individual person flowing along as water in the path of life set out by the true Way of nature. Each person is to do what he or she sees fit according to his or her own character and preference. This is not mere sensual self-indulgence, but instead is the ongoing realization of one's place in the flowing order of things. Harmony does not have to be constructed by human will, ingenuity, and artificial conformity—which is how the Daoists saw Confucianism. Harmony already exists in the Way of the natural world, and the enlightened person simply joins in that Way.

So the most important characteristic of the Daoist is ziran, naturalness, the quality of a thing just being itself. Water is an important symbol for Daoists, as it flows according to the path of things yet ultimately has its way upon all—as a waterfall, following the contours of the land, eventually reshapes those contours in its own smooth line. Indeed, the key term for Daoist action is, paradoxically, wu-wei, literally "nonaction" or, more exactly, "nonapparent action." The Daoist flows with the Dao and thus, in a basic sense, the Dao acts through him without him acting on his own. As the classic text of Daoism, the Dao De Ching, puts it:

In the pursuit of learning, every day something is acquired.
In the pursuit of Tao, every day something is dropped.

> Less and less is done.
> Until non-action is achieved.
> When nothing is done, nothing is left undone.
>
> The world is ruled by letting things take their course.
> It cannot be ruled by interfering.[8]

In the great, impersonal Dao, therefore, there is no thought and no feeling, and thus no passion for justice, compassion, love, and so on. The Daoist instead simply "rides the Dao" until death, and then wisely lets go of this life. There is no problem of God and evil in Daoism, for there is no God in any respect in which the problem of evil makes sense.

At about the same time that Kong-zi was formulating Confucianism and Daoist sages were arriving at their insights, young Śakyamuni Gotama Siddhārtha ("sage of the Śakya dynasty, of the lineage of Gotama, He-who-attains-the-goal-of-life") was considering the meaning of life.[9] According to the stories of his followers, he was born to the king of the Śakya kingdom in northeastern India. He descended from heaven, whence he had been residing because of the good deeds of his previous lives. The birth itself was miraculous (out of his mother's side) and painless, and was followed by predictions that he would become either a universal monarch or a Buddha (supreme sage).

His father, not surprisingly, preferred his son to succeed him on the throne. So the king did his best to isolate his son from the unhappiness of the world—the reality that typically drove many to religious reflection in India. He sought instead to keep him happy, comfortable, and contented. Young Siddhārtha thus grew up, enjoyed a fine education, and was married to the most beautiful princess, with whom he had a son.

One well-loved Buddhist narrative continues the story: "On a certain day he heard about the forests carpeted with tender grass. . . .When he heard of the delightful appearance of these parks beloved by the women, he resolved to go outdoors. He was like an elephant long shut up in a house." The king learned of it, and cried, "Heaven forbid that the prince with his tender nature should even imagine himself to be distressed." So the king had the roads cleared (although "with the greatest gentleness") of "all those who had mutilated limbs or maimed senses, the decrepit and the sick and all squalid beggars." Thus did the king attempt to preserve his son on the path the king preferred.

But as Siddhārtha set out, he saw an old man by the roadside. Siddhārtha asked his driver, "Who is this man that has come here, with white hair and his hand resting on a staff, his eyes hidden beneath his brows, his limbs bent down and hanging loose? Is this a change produced in him, or his natural state, or an accident?"

The charioteer candidly replied, "Old age has broken him down. It is the ravisher of beauty, the ruin of vigor, the cause of sorrow, the destruction of delights, the affliction of memories, the enemy of the senses. He too once drank milk in his childhood, and in time he learned to crawl on the ground. Having step by step become a vigorous youth, he has step by step in the same way reached old age."

The prince was astonished. "What! Will this evil come to me also?"

Yes, said the charioteer. "It will certainly come in time even to my long-lived lord. All the world knows that old age will destroy their beauty."

Siddhārtha then saw a sick man and had a similar conversation with his perhaps too-honest driver. Finally, on another trip, he beheld a dead man. Siddhārtha asked again, and the driver replied, "This is the final end of all living creatures. Be one a poor man, a man of middle state, or a noble, destruction will come to all in this world." Siddhārtha's reaction was instant: "He spoke with a loud voice, 'This is the end appointed to all creatures, and yet the world throws off all fear and is infatuated! The hearts of men must be hard, for they can be self-composed in such a situation.'" In these three sights, Siddhārtha recognized the problem of existence, *transience*: everything proceeds inexorably toward decay and disappearance. Nothing lasts forever.

Then he saw a fourth man, one who had renounced the world and retreated to the forest in order to concentrate upon spiritual things (thus a "renouncer," or *sannyāsīn*). So, in typical Indian style, Siddhārtha likewise tried the route of gurus and asceticism, leaving his throne, his palace, and his family. But soon he found that none of his spiritual leaders knew how to escape the cycle of rebirth, the endless round of reincarnation that could deliver neither a happy life on earth nor an eternal heaven of bliss—for one's merits, no matter how good and extensive, could not be more than finite, and thus eventually would fail to secure any lasting peace.

Siddhārtha then remembered that as a child he had once calmed himself by sitting beneath a tree in quiet. So he now did so and meditated, eating just enough to sustain his strength and keep him from distraction. Over time, he spiritually proceeded upward by stages. At last he achieved an utterly clear view of reality, full enlightenment (*bodhi*), and became the Buddha ("Enlightened One").

The earliest form of Buddhism is austere. Theravāda ("the tradition of the elders") teaches that there are no such things as deities or spirits. There is the world in its endless round of suffering and decay, and there is the path of enlightenment as taught by the Buddha, which promises the one and only escape from this treadmill of trouble. Buddhism most basically is a cure for a disease, a therapy for a problem, a release from a trap—it is eminently practical, not concerned with myths and metaphysics. Indeed, the original understanding of *nirvāṇa*—the attaining of which is the goal of each Buddhist—has nothing to do with happiness or pleasure. Instead, it is "where the candle flame goes when the candle is blown out." It is the dissolution of the self in the halting of desire. For the Buddha taught that desire breeds attachment and thus the fear of loss, and frustration over the goods one never gains. No desire, no fear. No desire, no frustration. No desire, no existence, no suffering. And, of course, no God to hurt or help, to condemn or to save, to answer to or call upon.

Such austerity, such a focus on the practical concerns of this life, is found in certain modern Western philosophies as well, although both the diagnosis of, and the remedy for, the human problem is quite different in each case. One such philosophy is positivism. Positivism is usually associated with the career of Auguste Comte. A nineteenth-century French sociologist, social reformer, and philosopher, Comte believed that human civilization had progressed through two previous stages of intellectual development, namely, religion and philosophy, and now was ready for full maturity: science. Science not only explained the natural world; it explained human life as well, Comte believed. Furthermore, science would furnish not just objective descriptions of reality, but also would somehow provide us with the guidelines along which the best human societies could be constructed. The idea of God, then, was an unhelpful holdover from a stage of human thought properly left behind. Human beings were to take adult responsibility for themselves in the cosmos. In Immanuel Kant's phrase, humanity had now "come of age."

This enthusiasm for reason—and for scientific reason above all—as the key to human fulfillment is shared by a more recent movement, secular humanism. John Dewey, Aldous Huxley, Isaac Asimov, and Carl Sagan are among those who have publicly identified with this position. As the two *Humanist Manifestoes* and the later *Secular Humanist Declaration* assert, human beings are on their own as governors of the planet (although there may be other intelligent beings elsewhere in the universe). The "secular" part of this philosophy's name denotes this belief that nothing supernatural exists with which we must contend or toward which we are responsible. The "humanist" part champions humanity as the highest of earthly beings and the measure of all good, the appropriate focus for all human endeavor. There is no God to blame for evil, no puzzle to work out. Human beings are the only conscious and moral agents on earth and must make their way as best they can according to the values they choose, aided particularly by the power of science and technology to create the future they desire.[10]

The central issue of God and evil, therefore, looks very different if one understands "God" differently. It also looks very different if one understands "evil" differently.

EVIL COULD BE OTHERWISE

Some theists, as well as some proponents of New Age thought, suggest that evil is really good. If one just looks at the world a certain way, so the idea goes, one can see that what looks like trouble, or even disaster, is really all for the best. Suffering builds character. Disappointment points us toward better choices. Illness concentrates our minds on the spiritual. And so on, and so on.

One can hardly argue with the proposition that good sometimes emerges out of evil. But as a comprehensive response to evil, it is inadequate. It seems not to take evil seriously enough. It underestimates the devastation of spirit and body that evil can cause. It ignores the many times when no obvious good, and certainly no *proportionate* good, balances and redeems the evil in question. In short, it tends to trivialize both evil and the suffering of those who endure it, even as it means instead to encourage such sufferers and those who care for them.

A quite different approach is to deal with evil as a perceptual problem. It's not so much that evil is really good, but rather that evil isn't real. Evil is just one illusion among the many that flow from the common, but mistaken, sense we all have that what is real is this desk, and that person, and this moment, and that event, and this pain, and that frustration. Instead, so certain forms of Indian religion (such as Advaita Hinduism and most varieties of Buddhism) suggest, we must strive to get beyond this world of appearances to perceive the true nature of ultimate reality, in which evil does not exist. Whether we penetrate to Brahman and merge with the One (as in Advaita Hinduism), or extinguish our desires and achieve *nirvāṇa* (as in Buddhism), we can leave evil behind in this world of false images and experiences.

A third alternative is to understand both "good" and "evil" as literal nonsense, as meaningless categories. Of course, three-year-old Devon may loudly pronounce chocolate to be "good" and vanilla to be "bad," but adults recognize with a smile that "good" and "evil" in this case are a matter of individual taste. (Although I myself am inclined to believe Devon may be on to a deep metaphysical truth.) In the same way, this is true for everything else in the cosmos at large—so this third alternative suggests. Human beings dislike pain and call it "evil." But strictly speaking, the designation "evil" implies a conviction that pain *ought not* to exist, and that when it does, it somehow marks a transgression of an objective order of goodness. Yet in several different worldviews, one's dislike of pain is just another instance of personal preference, rather than a meaningful judgment about the actual nature of things.

The world just is what it is. It contains things and events and experiences that some people prefer and others that some people do not. Native American religions generally accept the world as a great, comprehensive circle in which everything plays a role. Human beings are perfectly free to wish for more food rather than less, for more security against wild animals rather than less, and for more peace with their neighbors rather than less—but these are simply self-centered desires. They have nothing to do with the way things *ought* to be, because it is meaningless to say things ought to be anything other than what they are. The sensible person, therefore, spends no time wishing things were different and instead concentrates upon the demanding task of living as well as possible in the real world.

The modern philosophy of pragmatism makes a similar case. According to its exponents, ranging from William James to Richard Rorty, the world is simply a situation in which human beings make the best of life that they can. There are no absolute codes of ethics against which to measure choices, no divinely given standards of "right" and "wrong" or even "better" and "worse." There is just the world as we encounter it, to which we respond as we think best. Indeed, in James's famous phrase, the best ideas are those that have the highest "cash value." As James once wrote, "The whole function of philosophy ought to be to find out what definite difference it will make to you and me, at definite instants of our life, if this world-formula or that world-formula be the true one."[11] Notice that the fundamental concern here is not "what definite difference it will make" to God or the gods or some other transcendent order of goodness. The difference that counts is the difference to *us* in ways that we can measure and appreciate.

Various forms of existentialism have promoted this view at the individual level and in a radical way. Following certain insights of such diverse nineteenth-century thinkers as Søren Kierkegaard, Friedrich Nietzsche, and Fyodor Dostoyevsky, twentieth-century existentialists such as Albert Camus, Karl Jaspers, Simone de Beauvoir, and Jean-Paul Sartre championed individual self-determination. Indeed, Sartre's famous epigram that "existence precedes essence" means that human beings are thrown into the world and then pick themselves up, dust themselves off, and proceed to decide what they now are going to *be* through what they are going to *do*. For most of the prominent existentialists, there is no God (although Kierkegaard and Dostoyevsky themselves were Christians). There is no God, and no God-substitute, whether nation or religion or race or family, to *tell* anyone what to do. Each person actualizes himself or herself through consciously chosen action.

Each person makes of his or her life a statement, an artwork, a philosophy of life. In this worldview, evil remains only as a sort of residue from the Christian heritage of Europe. What is evil for these existentialists is "bad faith," by which they mean nothing to do with religious commitment, but rather mindless living in slavery to others' agendas rather than opting for the radical freedom offered by existentialism. To such existentialists, however, all choices are open without any objective standards of good or evil. As one critic of existentialism put it, one decides whether to help an old lady across a busy intersection or to run her down in one's car, but there is no moral judgment to attach to either choice as long as it is freely and firmly chosen.[12]

Of course, these sketches can only glance over the rich ideas of each religion and philosophy mentioned. And my main intention is not to assess these other viewpoints, but to explore the question of God and evil as it arises in theism and in Christian belief in particular. In the light of this brief survey, we must simply notice that there are other, deeply different, ways of approaching the whole matter of God/good and evil. Before we plunge into the problem of evil as it has been posed in Western intellectual and religious history, it is only right to acknowledge that the problem disappears, or is radically transformed, in other contexts.

THREE KINDS OF PROBLEMS

Still, the question of God and evil is an abiding problem for many people—it continues to be for me, too, even as I complete the final draft of this book. It is perhaps helpful to see that it can be a threefold problem.

First, it can be an *intellectual* problem, a sort of puzzle to be approached with ingenuity and insight. One has an intellectual problem if one's idea of God and one's idea of evil stand in some sort of awkward, even contradictory, relationship. So, for example, contemporary philosopher J. L. Mackie flatly asserts (as did Hume and Epicurus) that it is not logically possible to hold the three propositions that "God is good," "God is all-powerful," and "Evil exists" all at the same time. At least one of these ideas, Mackie insists, must give way.[13] Now an intellectual problem might well lead to a religious problem (as we shall see), but what we are identifying here is the problem of evil on the level of a sophisticated "game" or mental challenge, the sort of thing pursued in a highly formal way by philosophers.

Second, one has a *religious* problem if one's idea *and experience* of God (or ultimate reality, however understood) and one's idea *and experience* of evil seem importantly disjointed, or even at odds. Trevor can talk all night about the problem of evil at the intellectual level, and perhaps profitably, but he has a religious problem in this sense only if his fundamental understanding of and personal relationship toward ultimate reality are affected. It is good to see that this kind of problem can be acute for anyone. Atheists may find that, in the light of considering a strong case for faith in God despite the problem of evil, they come to doubt the nonexistence of God, just as theists can find it difficult in the face of troubling ideas or experiences to keep believing in God as all-good and all-powerful. Thus what I mean by the religious level is the level of *ultimacy*: how do we personally relate to whatever is finally real in the universe in the light of our ideas and experiences of evil? This is the "three-in-the-morning" level that involves our hearts as well as our heads.

There is a third level in-between these two, in which one's most basic convictions about reality are not seriously threatened, but at least some of one's intermediate values and actions are challenged. A person experiences an *existential* problem when ideas and experiences cast doubt on whether his or her pattern of life, or even a particular moral choice, is thoroughly in tune with his or her beliefs about God and evil. Perhaps Karen has blithely held a benign view of God's tolerance of evil, and she needs to take more seriously God's holiness and hatred of sin. Perhaps Ken has expected God always to rescue him from the consequences of selfish choices, but then serious disappointment shakes this overconfidence. Perhaps Michael has seen good and evil to be meaningless categories given the nonexistence of God or other objective moral reality, but then becomes a parent and is faced with the ethical education of his child. These instances are more than mere intellectual puzzles, but are also less than full-blown religious crises.

To resolve these problems, we theoretically have several options. First, we can endeavor to change our ideas or experiences of God. If the nature of evil seems indisputable, then perhaps God needs to be understood or experienced differently. Can we gain new ideas about God from books or other teachers? Are there communities or other social contexts that promote alternative experiences of God (including no-God)? Perhaps the atheist needs to read a sound book of Jewish theology, or the Christian needs to attend a Buddhist study group.

Second, if the nature of God seems clear, perhaps we need to change our idea or experience of evil. Again, are there opportunities for new insight or encounter? Perhaps the Muslim could listen to a powerful lecture on existentialism, or the positivist participate in a New Age celebration. The scholar could visit skid rows and nursing homes (as some do), and the social worker read some serious philosophy and theology (as some do).

Third, perhaps we need to change our understanding of the relationship between God and evil. Maybe God is more, or less, responsible for evil than we have previously thought. Maybe God is more, or less, involved in the world than we have previously experienced.

Finally, though, there is the possibility of changing the basic question at the heart of the issue. Perhaps the whole project of trying to nicely correlate our ideas and experiences of both God and evil is wrongheaded. Perhaps it is impossible, or just unhelpful. Perhaps we can better put another question to the heart of the matter. I think that this is, in fact, the case, and the last chapters of the book develop this possibility.

But before they do, the intervening chapters lay down some necessary groundwork. Most immediately, chapter 2 tries to set out just what theists mean by evil, in all its dimensions.

CHAPTER TWO

What Is Evil?

WE OUGHT TO BEGIN BY MAKING CLEAR what evil is *not*. Almost every time I discuss this issue, whether in university classes or public lectures or conversations over coffee, I come across the same assumption about the nature of evil. It shows up particularly in the common question, "Why did God create evil?"

There are respects in which this is a perfectly sensible question. But lurking within it, I believe, is a fallacy of what philosophers call "reification"—that is, a "making real" of what is actually only an abstraction. For evil is not a "something" that God could "create." It isn't a kind of molecule or virus or forcefield or giant black nebula that courses through the universe, infecting or affecting everything it encounters. There was no time when God said, "Let there be evil," and there was evil. Nor has evil been eternally existent as some sort of dualistic counterpart to God. There is, I maintain, no such thing as *evil*. Evil is primarily an adjective, and it becomes a noun only in the abstract. An action can be evil, or an event can be evil, or a quality can be evil, or a being can be evil. And we can lump all these particular evils together in our minds and come up with the category "evil." We can even go on to discuss it *as if it were* a particular thing, so long as we do not forget that we are always dealing with a category or group of particular evil things, not a thing itself.

What also lies behind the question "Why did God create evil?" are other, more appropriate, questions such as, "Why does God allow evil choices to be made in the first place?" and "Why did God create creatures who would make those evil choices?" and "Why did God create a world that seems full of evil events and conditions and relationships?" Most of this book responds to these good questions. First, however, we must set aside this common misconception that evil is a *stuff*, for the creation of which God must be called to account.[1]

As we turn to consider what evil *is*, we must distinguish the *subjective* from the *objective* understandings of evil. Evil, to particular subjects (such as you and me), is what we find, in a word, bad. It is not good. It is something that is other than it ought to be, as we judge things. It is not what we like or approve of or admire or prefer. "This is an evil-smelling perfume," we might say, and what we mean basically is that "I don't like it." We are not (unless we are thinking and speaking loosely) making a universal claim about its aromatic qualities. We are expressing merely our own preference.

As chapter 1 sketches briefly, this is all that some worldviews see evil to be. In many traditional native American cultures, for instance, "evil" is just what *we* do not enjoy, what diminishes *our* health or happiness or security. Nature is what it is. In contemporary philosophies (such as some forms of pragmatism, existentialism, and deconstruction), pronouncing something to be "evil" is to express merely one's individual values, or perhaps the values of one's group. For how can any of us, limited and flawed as we are, presume to pronounce infallibly upon the actual substance of a thing?

Sometimes, though, many of us will say that something is evil and we do intend to express more than our personal preference. Maria reads a news report about a particular crime, and her immediate response is that such an action was evil in and of itself. She is saying, in other words, that the crime is not just something she does not like (a *subjective* judgment), but that it is "just plain wrong." The crime is a deviation from some absolute standard of goodness. It *is* evil. Now, to think this sort of thing is to judge something to be evil *objectively*. When we speak this way, as we all do, we intend to say something about the object (that which we are calling evil), and not about the subject (ourselves) evaluating it.

Cornelius Plantinga borrows a line from the movie *Grand Canyon* to describe evil as "not the way it's supposed to be."[2] This is the fundamental objective understanding of evil. An order of goodness exists, and any deviation from it counts as evil. The ancient Hebrews had several terms for evil: crime, worthlessness, desecration, and others. The one used most in their Scriptures, however, means "to fall short of the mark," like an arrow that lands in the grass instead of reaching the target. Theists, such as Jews, Christians, and Muslims, identify this objective standard of goodness with the character and will of God. There is not some standard of goodness in the universe outside of God and against which God also is to be evaluated. God is the standard: God is good.

Human beings therefore know what is good and what is evil because God shares with us both this knowledge and this ability to judge. Many authors through history have remarked on the universal phenomenon of a conscience in human beings, an inner voice or marker that evaluates what *is* against what *ought* to be. In every culture, God also has given special wisdom to teachers who have helped to clarify the moral vision of their hearers. Even better, say the classic theistic faiths, God has empowered and commissioned prophets to set forth specific messages of divine revelation—whether the Hebrew prophets such as Samuel and Moses and Isaiah, whose messages are recorded in the Hebrew Bible; or Christian apostles such as Peter, John, and Paul, some of whose writings are traditionally believed to make up the New Testament; or Muḥammad, who received the words of God that were later recorded in the Qur'ān. Christians go beyond these other two faiths to claim, finally, that God became human in the person of Jesus of Nazareth, and thus gave a uniquely powerful revelation of what is good. Believers of certain other faiths, of course, dispute the idea that God was uniquely revealed in Jesus: Bahá'is would claim a similar status for Bahá'u'lláh, for instance, as would many Hindus for the avatars (or "manifestations") of the god Viṣṇu—such as Kṛṣṇa and Rāma. The main point here, however, is the claim of many religions that humans know about what is good and what is evil because God has revealed the objective standard: God's own character and activity.

A thoughtful reader might wonder whether theists thus have defined a conveniently circular situation that exempts God from any moral condemnation—that gets God off the hook, as it were, in the problem of evil. For if "good" is defined simply as "what God is and does," then by this definition God cannot be or do evil, and that's that. We might *subjectively* judge something to be evil, but if God is responsible for it, then it must *objectively* be good, and we ought to change our views as best we can to fit with this reality. Thus the problem of evil "disappears" by verbal sleight of hand.

In response to this, first, we must recognize that, yes, such theism does say that we ought to learn what is good and what is evil from God. It also says that human beings ought actively to improve our sense of morality by conforming it to God's revealed standard. On our own, we have badly flawed understandings of morality and need God to reorient them.

Second, however, God is not let off the hook, or out of the dock, quite so easily. For the question of "God and evil" is posed, after all, by theists themselves, not just by others. Indeed, sometimes the question is posed most sharply by believers precisely because they are utterly depending, body and soul, on the goodness of God. And the question is basically this: doesn't God seem scandalously inconsistent, since the world seems scandalously inconsistent? However pious the believer, however much one determines to develop a moral code in full congruity with God's revealed character and activity, the world yet seems full of moral contradictions. Thus one cannot derive a consistent ethic from the available phenomena around us. In short, *whatever* the divine definition of goodness is, God seems manifestly not to keep to it in God's own work in the world. And inconsistency of this radical sort makes any objective understanding of good and evil apparently impossible. Thus the proposition "God is good" turns out to be a meaningless affirmation, as "good" becomes a redundancy on the end of the stark proposition that "God is."

The rest of this chapter attempts to outline the many forms in which this question of God's inconsistency is posed in the context of our encounter with evil. Let us begin here with the instances of evil that even institutions as secular as insurance companies have called "acts of God."

NATURAL EVIL

Let us begin by granting that as we look at the world, nature often seems terrible. The earth itself throws up volcanoes and earthquakes. The atmosphere can be too hot or too cold for any life to thrive, too windy or too still, too wet or too dry. Plants and animals act as parasites or predators, and species suffer from over- or underpopulation. Finally, the heavens themselves send down meteorites, solar flares, radiation, and other dangers. Some of these features of nature may not be evil in themselves. But sometimes they pose threats to living things that might well be classed as evil.

Not only does nature seem terrible: it also seems, well, imperfect. It seems makeshift and even wasteful. Evolutionists from Darwin himself to contemporary neo-Darwinists such as Stephen Jay Gould have seen in nature both powerful confirmation of evolution by natural selection and corresponding evidence for the lack of divine supervision of such a process. Gould points to the so-called panda's thumb with which the panda scrapes bark off bamboo in order to eat the tender shoots within. This "thumb," however, is not a digit at all, but a wrist bone extended to serve as a rough implement for this task. Gould is confident that no divine engineer would have produced a mechanism so crude, if adequate: a blind, impersonal process such as evolution makes much better sense: "Odd arrangements and funny solutions are the proof of evolution—paths that a sensible God would never tread."[3]

The panda's thumb presents a rather benign form of this argument. After all, the panda does seem to get along rather well with this device, so how does a paleontologist presume to judge it unworthy of a Supreme Being? Other creatures, however, do not get along so well. David Hume, a hundred years before Darwin, pointed to the parsimony of nature that seemed to apportion to creatures just enough resources and abilities to survive, but with little of what we might in our age call "redundancy systems." Like a strict master rather than an indulgent parent, wrote Hume, nature has gifted its offspring grudgingly, and mistakes or unanticipated threats have deadly consequences for such precarious existences.

Darwin extended this idea by remarking on a sort of paradox: nature might be parsimonious with particular beings, but it was prodigal with groups and even whole species so that competition for resources ensued. Nature seems to set "all against all," in Thomas Hobbes's phrase, so that only the fittest survive. Consumption of life by life, and not infrequently by startling forms of parasitism and predation, is so common in nature as to constitute an essential part of its order. Indeed, the mechanism of natural selection, the key to Darwin's model of how evolution progresses, arises out of his observations of such competition among various modes of survival in changing environments. In short, Darwinian evolution presupposes an obvious, and crucial, fact of life in the natural world: there is a lot of suffering and death. Christian thinkers also wonder about this as they consider how God might have created the world via evolution. If God did so, they muse, then what does this gigantic chain of struggle and misery and death say about God's providence? As one of Darwin's biographers puts it, "What was one to think of a God, supposedly benevolent, supposedly paternal, who created entire species, allowed them to flourish for a while, then wiped them out?"[4]

Darwinian evolution can be seen, therefore, as a response to a form of the problem of evil: the manifold evils in nature. And in Darwin's case, his ruminations upon what he observed during his famous trip on the *Beagle*, as well as his other scientific studies, ultimately eroded his Christian faith. Darwin had trained for the Anglican priesthood at Cambridge, but he later publicly averred an agnosticism that, in the eyes of most of his biographers, amounted finally to a diffident atheism.[5] And a not-so-diffident atheism marks the work of many influential Darwinians today, such as Gould and Richard Dawkins—both of whose popular writings are shot through with atheistic affirmations.[6]

In sum, the inefficiency, wastefulness, suffering, and death of the natural world prompts many to wonder about the goodness and power of God.

MORAL EVIL

Many treatments of the question of evil distinguish between natural and moral evil. Natural evil is no one's "fault" (except maybe God's, as in "acts of God") because no moral agent effects it. Animal, vegetable, and mineral simply act according to their natures, and sometimes evil things happen. Or at least things happen that *from some points of view seem* evil, whether imperfect, wasteful, painful, or even disastrous. Moral evil, on the other hand, is called this precisely because it *is* someone's fault: the fault of the morally responsible agent who performs it.[7]

Immediately, however, we must consider a qualification of this neat distinction. For yes, evil can be *intentional*: Carolyn intends to strike Bob on the head because she is angry with him. But evil can also be *accidental*: while retrieving her briefcase from the airplane overhead bin, Carolyn unintentionally strikes Bob on the head. And evil can also be *ironic*, having precisely the opposite (or at least another) effect than the one intended: a wasp is buzzing around Bob's head, and as Carolyn attempts to protect her friend by swatting the wasp with a newspaper, she strikes poor Bob, once again, on the head.

When we consider actions by moral agents we now have two levels of analysis, not one. We want to know both what was the evil that resulted from an action, but also what was the motive of the effecting party. To assess the overall "evil" of a situation, then, we must take both levels into account—as does a court of law.

Cornelius Plantinga complicates things further by pointing to the reality of "involuntary evil," which results from evil character, from patterns of sinfulness woven so deeply into a person's life that evil behavior becomes "natural":

Involuntary sins are surprisingly common. For example, the seven deadly sins (pride, envy, anger, sloth, avarice, gluttony, and lust) are usually involuntary. They are desires, beliefs, and attitudes over which a person may have little or, at best, only variable control. . . . Where the deadly sins are concerned, a person may not want these states of mind (*nobody* wants to be envious), may not choose them, may not mean or try to have them. In fact, just the contrary. Yet there they are.[8]

Furthermore, taking motive into account raises the issue of God and evil in a more nuanced way. For there might be something appropriate in God's allowing a moral agent to perform an action he or she fully intends to perform. But it seems a quite different matter for God to allow evil to result from accidents, and even more difficult to understand why God would allow evil to result when the moral agent actually intends to do good.

A second order of distinction customarily differentiates between evil done to *oneself* and evil done to *others*. Suicide may or may not be a crime or a sin, but homicide seems certainly to be both. Less dramatically, it is one thing to deny oneself food: perhaps one is trying to lose weight, or fasting, or engaging in a scientific study. Perhaps instead one is torturing oneself or even committing slow suicide. It is quite another thing, however, to deny someone else food without consulting her about her preference, *even in* the morally more ambiguous cases of dieting or science. It is a serious question why God allows people to harm themselves. It is, if anything, an even more serious question why God allows people to harm others.

A third distinction is between *individual* evil and *corporate* evil. Most of the examples so far have dealt with individuals acting in an evil way. But groups can act in evil ways as well. Gang or mob violence is an obvious example. Death squads, embezzlement conspiracies, treasonous cabals are others. Even cartels and political pork barrels generally are seen to be wrong. Groups can act badly, and while sociologists work hard to specify comprehensively just why this occurs, it seems clear that sometimes groups act even worse than their constituent members might act on their own.[9]

Finally, there are *particular instances* of evil and there are *systems* of evil. Gary loses his temper once in a while and scares the children with violent shouting. Each of those losses of self-control, each of those moments of terror for the children, is an evil. But if Gary *habitually* upsets the family through shouting, if the children anxiously cower or lie in order to divert his verbal storm, if Gary's spouse fails to protect the children in order to preserve herself from his fury, then the whole family is afflicted with *systemic* evil. Religious communities, neighborhoods, companies, and governments all can be twisted and dominated by evil in their very nature. Evil isn't an occasional product of such a group; it is in the very fiber and structure of the organization. How, then, can God allow both particular instances of sin and whole complexes, entire self-perpetuating systems—even, as it were, *organisms*—of sin?

The category of moral evil expands significantly if one accepts the historic teaching of all three major theistic faiths that human beings and God are not the only moral agents in the cosmos. Putting aside the question of whether animals have morality (there is little to go on in this regard, whether in zoology or in classical theology), the traditional theistic religions assert the existence of evil spirits.

Judaism and Christianity teach explicitly that evil spirits, led by the archfiend Satan, conspire against the rule of God and the good of the world, and especially of humankind. Islam speaks of the jinn, some of whom are evil and serve Satan, or Iblīs. As in Judaism and Christianity, these powerful and malignant creatures once were good. Jews and Christians see the evil beings as "fallen angels," or former spiritual servants of God. These evil angels, or demons, rebelled against God's sovereignty at some point in the remote past and have since been engaged in an unrelenting campaign to frustrate, if not destroy, God's work of blessing the world. Islam says that Satan refused God's command to honor humanity at its creation, and thus began his career of antagonism. For all three faiths, then, the cosmos includes not only God, human beings, animals, plants, and the rest, but also angels and demons or jinn, who are engaged in a spiritual war that has Earth as its battlefield.[10]

Judaism, Christianity, and Islam all reject the theological concept of dualism—the idea that God and Satan are exact counterparts, one a good spirit and the other an evil spirit, equal in power and locked in a cosmic struggle. God alone is self-existent, they maintain, and keeps everything else in existence. Thus even the devil himself depends upon God's sustaining power to continue existing. And all three faiths are confident that God will triumph over evil at the end of history, dealing once and for all with the devil and his minions.

Satan is not the "opposite" of God, not God's mirror image. Let's go on in this vein to clear away a few more popular myths about Satan. Satan is not the source of all evil, for Satan does not possess comprehensive knowledge or power. Evil choices are made by human beings without those choices always being traceable to (and thus blameable upon) Satan. Nor does Satan have his own private head-quarters in hell, as is so often pictured in cartoons both modern and medieval. Most traditions of Judaism, Christianity, and Islam assert that Satan in fact is destined for hell, the place of radical separation from God, and this is the only respect in which Satan is identified with hell. (There is some hint in the Qur'ān that Satan himself might be redeemed: see especially sura 15. There is no similar hint in the Jewish or Christian Scriptures.) Instead of being the prince of hell, Satan temporarily enjoys the status of the "prince of this world," according to the New Testament. This term signifies a grim recognition that Satan has considerable influence over individuals, corporations, and structures throughout the world in this era. This influence causes much harm, but it will also end by God's direct intervention in history in the Last Judgment.

All this talk of supernatural beings and spiritual warfare and heavens and hells can seem peculiar, even anachronistic, to many thoughtful people in modern cultures. How can intelligent people take seriously the possibility of spirit beings who wreak evil in the world?

The lore of Judaism, Christianity, and Islam is full of speculation, but only a small core of instructive material appears in the authoritative Scriptures themselves. We seem to have two ways of judging the reality of such beings. The first would be to assess the credibility of the sources that claim the existence of angels and demons. Can the Hebrew Scriptures, or Christian Bible, or Muslim Qur'ān be trusted in this regard?

The second way would be to examine the phenomenon of evil in the world and attempt to decide whether natural causes alone suffice to explain the quantity and quality of such evil. Do some individual or corporate evils, even systems of evil, seem more wicked than one would have thought human beings alone capable of producing? A number of people with a wide range of beliefs have come to believe that our times truly have been haunted by what these people have come to call "the demonic"—whether the evils under Hitler, Stalin, and Pol Pot on a huge scale, or the torture and murder of innocents by serial killers on the individual scale—even as many of them cannot embrace traditional religious teaching about demons literally.[11]

The small core of instructive material in the Scriptures about such beings is adamant that these spiritual foes exist and act. In each religion, however, the person who wishes to make spiritual progress is directed not to be preoccupied with fighting the devil, but rather with loving God. Struggle with evil—whether natural, human, or demonic—is an inescapable part of making one's way through a deeply troubled world. But the primary goal is the positive one of a beautiful relationship with God and God's good creation, not the negative one of victory over enemies.

Though a detailed treatment of spiritual evil can be important in its own terms, the central question in our inquiry is the nature of the relationship between God and these evil beings, and thus between God and what these evil beings do. Is God responsible, and how is God responsible, for their creation and continued existence? Is God responsible, and how is God responsible, for the effects of these malignant creatures in the cosmos?

NATURAL AND MORAL EVIL IN HUMANITY

George Bernard Shaw quipped that the statistics on death were quite impressive: one out of every one persons dies. He might have said the same thing about sin. Theologians, poets, philosophers, psychologists, pastors, and social workers all have wrestled with the apparent fact of universal sin and with the question of its origins. Are human beings corrupt at birth or even at conception? Do we instead learn sin inevitably, shaped as we are by corrupt social structures? Are both nature and nurture, heredity and environment, involved? Because human beings are not simply bodies and not simply souls (according, at least, to Jewish, Christian, and Muslim conceptions of humanity), sorting out physical and spiritual causes and effects is a challenge. As Hans Schwarz has commented, "Because human behavior is subject to genetic and physical influences, one cannot strictly distinguish between natural and moral evil."[12]

Most of us think it is appropriate to seek the causes of behavior in order to make moral judgments, in order to assess responsibility for one's actions. Our courts often find someone has indeed committed a crime but then sends the defendant to counseling rather than prison. They find such a person not guilty, not culpable, because some physical cause—whether a drug, or a brain lesion, or a genetic anomaly, or some other physical agent affecting consciousness—reduced this person's ability to make good moral choices to the point that normal responsibility for the decision in question cannot be expected.

One recent argument asserts that homosexuality is as valid an expression of human bonding as heterosexuality because it results from particular physical causes during a person's gestation. Homosexuality must therefore be all right, that is, because it is provided by nature and not by moral choice. Others suggest, however, that alcoholism and other drug abuse, violence to self or others, and other behaviors that our culture does not judge tolerable may have genetic roots as well. Those born with such predispositions might well be judged to be less "culpable" for any transgressions they might commit, but they are nonetheless expected to strive to conform to societal norms of healthy behavior.

The point here is not, of course, to suggest an answer to these various debates. It is only this: sorting out moral issues for human beings requires taking seriously the categories of both the natural/physical and the moral because we are psychosomatic (body and soul) units.

DEGREES OF EVIL

The problem of God and evil can be posed in three distinct degrees. First, does not *any* evil at all seem inconsistent with the idea of God? If God is all-good and all-powerful, and God made everything, then the slightest blemish in creation seems inconsistent. Now, such a perfect world, or even a slightly marred alternative, seems a very long way from our badly troubled globe, so this question appears rather academic. But it is a crucial one: why is there any evil at all?

As we move on to the world as it actually is, it is obvious that there is in fact a *lot* of evil in this world. Can we really believe in God in the face of *this much* evil? Surely philosophers who have tried to argue that this is "the best of all possible worlds" have been badly mistaken. Surely we see around us, every day, multiple instances of evil that God could ameliorate or even remove without resulting in any evident corollary harm.

David Hume reflected upon this, and recognized that perhaps God could not always suspend natural law whenever someone decided to do something foolish, such as drive a vehicle too fast around a bend. If such behavior had no likely evil consequences, people would drive any way they liked, and we soon would have an utterly fantastic world of vehicles careering this way and that with all sorts of supernatural interventions to prevent harm being done. It is impossible to imagine, in fact, what sort of world this would be.

But for now, at least, we can follow Hume's logic to ask why God would not at least *occasionally* suspend those rules, or persuade the person not to drive so fast in the first place, or cause a tire to deflate before the person reached a dangerous speed? Furthermore, wrote Hume, granted that we can regulate our behavior by observing the function of natural laws and, that such order in the universe is a good, what about *freak* accidents? In the nature of the case, a freak accident cannot be predicted (at least not by human beings) on the basis of our knowledge of natural laws. So whatever good comes from living in a regulated universe cannot be gained in such instances. Therefore, he asked, why doesn't God prevent at least *them*?[13]

Such accidents belong to what philosophers call the third degree, *gratuitous* evil. One contemporary writer recalls being roused from sleep in a cabin. Screams issued from the woods as an animal was slowly killed and devoured, and then finally they ceased. This horrible experience, he writes, confirmed his atheism. Predation was bad enough. But the prolonged torture of this innocent animal for *no good reason at all* was too much. Surely no good and powerful God could allow this instance of suffering, much less condone such an event as part of the normal workings of nature.[14]

When presented with this story in terms of a deer attacked by wolves, one of my students suggested that the suffering of the deer might not have been gratuitous after all. Perhaps its cries accomplished the good of warning away other deer from the ravening wolf pack, while a mercifully quick death would have left the other deer vulnerable.[15] This suggestion points to a major line of theistic argument: what might appear to be gratuitous evil is not necessarily without good result—we just don't see the good, and so mistakenly conclude that there is none. This argument is, strictly speaking, an argument to a stalemate with the critic: no limited human being can know whether any evil is in fact gratuitous.

Still, the evidence for gratuitous evil at least *seems* strong: whether it is a child suffering yet another beating from a vicious parent, or a slave laboring yet another day in bondage, or another dissident newspaper being suppressed yet again by a totalitarian state—what possible good can *these* do? How can God allow them each and all?[16]

And so we round up our questions. Why did God create a world to which evil seems endemic? Why does God continue to allow—or even cause?—natural evils to occur? Why did God create beings capable of evil moral choices? And why does God continue to allow such choices to be made and their consequences to persist? Finally, if God is ultimately responsible for everything that exists—since nothing exists without God's sustaining power and, therefore, consent—then why is there any evil at all? Why is there this much evil? And why is there evil that seems to be utterly gratuitous?

As if these questions weren't enough to occupy us, though, several further questions, tightly related to these, deserve attention before we begin to consider and formulate responses.

CHAPTER THREE

Further Problems

GUILTY VERSUS INNOCENT

To be guilty of something and get one's "just deserts" is one thing. Yet all around us, the guilty prosper and the innocent suffer. Crime, all too often, pays quite handsomely. And virtue seems to be, indeed, its only reward.

This is hardly an observation unique to our times, of course. In the Hebrew Scriptures believers cried out to a God who, they believed, hated injustice and took the side of the oppressed. The prophet Habakkuk represents many others down history's pain-filled halls:

> O LORD, how long shall I cry for help, and you will not listen? Or cry to you "Violence!" and you will not save? . . . So the law becomes slack and justice never prevails. The wicked surround the righteous—therefore judgment comes forth perverted. (Habakkuk 1:2,4 NRSV)

Jeremiah echoes this lament:

> Why does the way of the guilty prosper? Why do all who are treacherous thrive? You plant them, and they take root; they grow and bring forth fruit; you are near in their mouths yet

far from their hearts. . . . How long will the land mourn, and the grass of every field wither? For the wickedness of those who live in it the animals and the birds are swept away, and because people said, "He is blind to our ways." (Jeremiah 12:1–2, 4 NRSV)

Yet when such a cry is raised, it raises also some important questions. To begin, who shall be reckoned to be among the "guilty"? According to what standard shall the kind and degree of guilt be assessed? Who is qualified and empowered to perform the reckoning? And how should those who are found guilty be most appropriately treated? If the concept of guilt and the ideal of justice are to have meaning beyond one's personal preference or advantage ("Help me, O God, because I don't like the situation in which others have placed me"), then these transcendent questions must be asked and answered well.

The opposite term, "innocent," is also not without its conceptual and practical difficulties. Who is innocent? Of what, and in what sense? According to what standard? And who is to judge? Perhaps, for instance, one is innocent in the sense of "not having had anything to do with X, and so not deserving the consequences of X." But perhaps one is guilty of Y, and X is a form of retribution for committing Y. Or perhaps one is not as innocent of X as it seems at first glance. . . .

When we speak of guilt and innocence, and particularly when we protest that guilt is not punished nor innocence protected and blessed, we generally do not mean to speak only subjectively. We do not mean to express merely our own preferences about how people ought to behave. Our instinct is to pronounce this rapist or that extortionist, or this reckless driver or that murderous thief, *objectively* guilty, whether or not a court finds him guilty, whether or not he gets away with his misdeed. Yet we might want to pause over that instinct for justice. How do we come to such conclusions about evil behavior and its practitioners? How do we have such confidence in our moral judgment? Some might protest that it is rather imperious of us to impose our moral standards on another human being. Isn't morality simply a matter of convention? Isn't it simply the product of a society's history and its current power relations?

Well, what do we make of the categories of guilt and innocence, of the concept of justice? Where do such ideas come from, and where *ought* they to come from? If we can answer these basic questions, then (and perhaps only then) we are properly poised to ask questions about God's apparently inept or uncaring response to injustice in the world. If we cannot answer them, however, then perhaps we ought to leave off accusing God for a while and think harder about what we do mean by guilt and innocence. Things may not be as straightforward as we think they are.

Still . . . still . . . there are some encounters with evil before which we ought to philosophize only with trembling. Elie Wiesel has written for the millions of Jews and other victims of the Nazi Holocaust, and we listen to him in silent deference:

> Never shall I forget that night, the first night in camp, which has turned my life into one long night, seven times cursed and seven times sealed. Never shall I forget that smoke. Never shall I forget the little faces of children, whose bodies I saw turned into wreaths of smoke beneath a silent blue sky.
>
> Never shall I forget those flames which consumed my faith forever.[1]

Some questions of guilt and innocence surely are beyond dispute.

INCONSISTENCY

A related problem, but a different one, is that of inconsistency. Only the most bitter cynic would claim that *all* of the wicked prosper *always*, and *all* of the righteous suffer *always*. *Some* guilty people seem to flourish with impunity, while others do get justice. Some innocents suffer, but others are rescued, and still others lead blessed lives untouched by trouble.

Why is this so? Why are we confronted with this weird mixture, with a world that manifests certain structures of justice, and yet also presents strong and enduring patterns of injustice? Why this massive inconsistency in which honesty sometimes is truly the best policy—even financially or politically—and sometimes isn't?

This inconsistency can perplex believers who search the world for clues to God's character and ways. For sometimes a moral order is evident. Sometimes things work out the way we think they ought to work out, and we breathe a sigh and pronounce with Browning that "God's in his heaven; all's right with the world." We must not be so preoccupied with evil as to forget that all over the world human beings have believed that they have discerned a fundamental moral "way" in the universe, and concluded that things are not ultimately chaotic and absurd.[2] Many religions and philosophies affirm this moral order. Much of what is so distressing about evil is precisely that it seems so at variance with this good order, with this better, even perfect, way that often comes into view, only to disappear again behind a cloud of grief, or sin, or confusion.

If sin always paid off, if virtue always failed, then we would have a serious, and probably overwhelming, problem with the idea that a good and powerful God is directing the cosmos. But that is not the situation we face. We face instead a tremendously inconsistent world, which evidences at once both a beautiful moral order, but also a hideous nightmare of successful perversity. This doubleness in reality is what led wise ones in many cultures to conclude that there is evil in the gods themselves, or that dualism exists at the highest level of being, or that this contradictory world is not finally real, and ultimate reality lies in something beyond. What can theists, who cannot accept such options, sensibly make of it?

THE PROBLEM OF MEANING

The only serious philosophical question is suicide, asserted French novelist and Nobel laureate Albert Camus almost half a century ago. Is life worth living or not?[3]

The problem of meaning is about life itself, and about all of its constituent parts and moments. Not only my life in *toto*, but my job, my relationships, my aspirations, my disappointments, my art, my work on behalf of others: does any of this actually mean anything? Does it matter? Is the whole human story not a coherent narrative at all, but ultimately just so much "sound and fury, signifying nothing"?

Some philosophers point out that the problem of meaning is more basic than the problem of evil. At the intellectual level, if there is no meaning to anything, then the problem of evil falls away into absurdity: it doesn't mean anything either. At the existential and religious level, the problem of meaning is basic, too. If there is meaning to the cosmos, and if evil itself somehow can be seen to have meaning—if it has some intelligible place in the order of things—then perhaps evil can be endured and even significantly resisted. Perhaps, indeed, there is a God behind, and in, it all that can let us in on the significance of things, even of evil. The worst possible answer for the theist to the problem of God and evil, taken on its own, is that God is either not entirely good or not entirely powerful. But if there is no meaning, then by definition there is no God at all.[4]

The close relation between the problem of meaning and the problem of evil is not, however, evident only to careful philosophical scrutiny. It is at the heart of the elementary human cry in the face of evil: "*Why?*" This question leaps up in every heart. Meaning is important to us. We cannot live without it. We want to believe that our suffering as well as our success actually *means something*. A striking exchange in Ingmar Bergman's film *The Seventh Seal*, speaks for many of us:

Knight: I want knowledge, not faith, not suppositions, but knowledge. I want God to stretch out his hand toward me, reveal Himself and speak to me.

Death: But he remains silent.

Knight: I call out to him in the dark but no one seems to be there.

Death: Perhaps no one is there.

Knight: Then life is an outrageous horror. No one can live in the face of death, knowing that all is nothingness.[5]

It is interesting to ask what we mean (!) by all this. Is it that we want our lives to count for eternity—is this a version of the human desire for immortality? Do we fear that, like Shelley's once-great Ozymandias, "king of kings," all that we have lived and worked for, all that we have loved and treasured, will collapse and disappear as ruins in the sands of time? If we do, furthermore, *why* do we fear this? Why should we care so much about leaving an imprint on the universe? Perhaps we are just overweening egomaniacs who ought, instead, to live just for the moment and then let it go—as Daoism and existentialism in their different ways would affirm. Or does this desire for lasting cosmic significance hint at a reality that corresponds to it? Is there an afterlife after all?

THE PROBLEM OF GOOD

In discussions of the problem of evil, some overlook the related point that *good* needs to be explained every bit as much as does evil. Of course, one should ask what the words "good" and "evil" actually mean. More comprehensively, though, the actual experience of good needs understanding. The three categories we used for "degrees of evil" can help here as well.

First, why is there *any* good at all? Why isn't the world unremittingly evil? This question, for theism, instantly brings to light one of the basic differences between good and evil. Evil is not merely the opposite of good. It is always in some way derivative of good, whether by living off of good or by perverting good. What would an entirely evil planet look like? Perhaps a hunk of rock in space, such as the asteroids between Mars and Jupiter? Or a planet with a life-destroying atmosphere? Yet even these instances, of course, have their beauties, and perhaps other goods as well, such as energy sources as yet untapped. Can one, then, imagine a world that is evil in *every aspect*? Can one imagine *anything* as totally evil? I cannot, and I have not encountered in science, philosophy, or literature any description of such a world.

This makes the question of "Why is there good?" come close to "Why is there anything at all?" They are not necessarily the same question, since whether existence itself is a good is a vexed philosophical debate. But beyond sheer existence, it is difficult to think of something as having no other good qualities, if only in potentiality. So why is the cosmos this way?

It is worth pausing at this point, furthermore, to tackle a question that comes up often in this discussion. Doesn't the existence of good *require* somehow the existence of evil? Aren't they related, like light and shadow—perhaps even beautifully, at some level, as in a painting by Rembrandt? Even if they aren't related positively, does not the existence of good entail the existence of evil?

No, it doesn't. But this common question is not completely wrongheaded. It makes, instead, what philosophers call a "category mistake." It talks about actual *existence*, when it should talk about *concepts*. It may well be, that is, that the *concept* of "good" does not make sense unless it includes the idea of the alternative, "evil"—and vice versa. I myself cannot think of a way to define good that does not at least imply the concept of evil, the "not-good," the "otherwise." But the *existence* of a good universe, with no evil beings and no evil actions and no evil events, seems entirely possible. Evil is not in any way necessary to the proper functioning of a universe. Indeed, evil by definition marks a *malfunction* of a universe. Good probably *has* to exist for there to be anything at all. (Remember, of course, that "good" and "evil" are abstractions for particular good things, ideas, qualities, etc.) Indeed, something good has to be there for evil to do something bad to or with it. Evil is always derivative, and thus does not *necessarily* exist.[6]

The next level of questioning pushes us much further to considering the presence of *this much* good in the world. The fact is, there is a lot of good in the world. How do we explain it? Is it the result of randomness, or of mathematical and physical regularities playing themselves out? Is it all impersonal and "just so"?

Consider how we feel in the presence of evil. We may feel fear, of course, or disgust, or other unpleasant emotions. But basic to most people's reaction to evil is rage at what seems so *wrong*, so unnecessary and deviant and hurtful. And if we believe there is a God, many of us feel angry at this God and blame God, even curse God, for the evil we experience. Now let's consider the opposite situation, a situation of delight. Whether in a holiday spent with loving relatives, a success shared with colleagues, a victory celebrated with teammates, a rescue shared with emergency workers, or a work of art appreciated with fellow admirers—why do many human beings report a spontaneous feeling of *thankfulness* welling up within them? Not just thankfulness to one's human associates, but a gratitude reaching beyond to—to what? Or to whom? Perhaps (as Feuerbach and Freud contended) this thankfulness is merely the psychological projection of parental figures onto the blank screen of a silent, impersonal cosmos, a pathetic figment of an immature imagination. But we owe it to ourselves to ask seriously whether our reaction in fact points to a reality, whether something or someone is truly there to be thanked for the good in our lives.

Finally, why is there *gratuitous* good: good that seems to do no important "good" at all? In the words of the slogan of civic-minded activists, what about "random acts of kindness and senseless beauty"? Why be generous or compassionate? Where does beauty, and our ability to apprehend and enjoy beauty, come from? It is one thing to argue that a flower is colored and shaped the way it is in order to attract certain insects for the purposes of pollination. It is another thing, though, to ponder why we humans find it beautiful—it seems a sheer bonus.

In sum, every explanation of the world that attempts to account for evil must also take full account of good. It will not do, for instance, to adopt a cynical attitude of dismissing the world as only and everywhere awful, because it isn't. One will have to decide for oneself whether it makes the most sense, as some religions suggest, to see the good in the world as just so much illusion or distraction. Other philosophies contend that classic virtues or beautiful features are nothing other than biological advantages. Thus some evolutionists echo the assertions of those ideologies—from native religions to pragmatic philosophies—which suggest that all the things we call "good" are in fact part of an amoral order of things: it is just our own preferences that lead us to call them good, to place value on one thing over its alternative. So, we must ask ourselves, is this all there is to "good"?

Whatever one's verdict, though, much remains to be explained in the categories of both "good" and "evil."

CONCLUSION

Any response to evil worthy of serious consideration must deal with both natural and moral evil—and possibly supernaturally caused evil as well. It must acknowledge the various degrees of evil. Any serious response to evil must also consider the related problems of evil in the lives of both the guilty and the innocent, and the phenomenon of inconsistency. Finally, it must respond to the problems of meaning and of the existence of good. Whether it deals with each of these individually in turn, or suggests a response that covers them all, an adequate response will leave none of them aside.

PART TWO

Responses

CHAPTER FOUR

Other Angles

IN THIS CHAPTER, OUR DISCUSSION MOVES
away from posing questions and toward considering responses. As a
sort of transit from one to the other, we can examine several themes
that place the issue of God and evil in new perspective.

THIS WORLD AND THE NEXT

Are this life and this world all there is? If there is no afterlife, then any
response to the problem of evil must "work" within this world and
this life.[1] Religions of Indian origin generally teach that the life we
currently live is only a single episode in a long-running series of lives
past and future. So questions of good and evil in Hinduism, Buddhism, and Jainism are resolved over a very long timeline. From this
point of view, then, it would be absurd to try to understand the workings of good and evil by looking only at the present life of an individual or the present state of the cosmos.

Judaism, Christianity, and Islam, however, posit just one earthly
life per human being. They also all affirm the reality of an ultimate
judgment upon each human life and a subsequent eternal state that
depends on the outcome of that judgment. The religions disagree

with each other, and groups within each also disagree, about the nature of the judgment and the character of the resulting states of existence. All agree, however, that an afterlife follows the consummation of this world and of each particular human life within it. For these theisms, any approach to the question of God and evil must keep this reality in view.

This reality is implicitly denied in a well-known passage in Fyodor Dostoyevsky's *The Brothers Karamazov*. Ivan Karamazov describes the pitiful state of a young man, Richard, who was raised by shepherds in what we would today call a situation of neglect and abuse. Richard later turned to a life of petty crime and drunkenness. Then he robbed and killed an old man, was caught, and was condemned to die. Christians throughout the city flocked to him, says Ivan, teaching him to read and write and pressing the Christian religion upon him until, at last, Richard made a public profession of conversion and a public confession of his capital crime. At this point his Christian supporters rejoiced in his eternal salvation while condemning his crimes and endorsing his eventual execution. Ivan's sarcasm is heavy:

> All who were of elevated station and good breeding rushed to
> see him in prison; Richard was kissed, embraced: "You are our
> brother, grace has come upon you!" And Richard himself only
> piously wept: "Yes, grace has come upon me! Before, all my
> childhood and youth, I would fain have eaten of the husks that
> the swine did eat, yet now grace has come upon me, and I die
> in the Lord!" "Yes, yes, Richard, die now in the Lord, you have
> shed blood and must die in the Lord. Even though you are not
> to blame for being wholly ignorant of the Lord at all at the
> time when you envied the swine their husks and when you
> were flogged for stealing their husks from them (which was a
> bad thing to do, for stealing is not permitted), you have shed
> blood and must die." And then his last day arrived. The un-
> nerved Richard wept and could do nothing but repeat every
> moment: "This is the finest day of my life, I am going to the
> Lord!" "Yes," cried the pastors, the judges and the charitable

ladies, "this is your happiest day, for you are going to the Lord!" All these people made their way to the scaffold behind the cart of shame in which Richard was being taken there, in carriages, on foot. Then they attained the scaffold: "Die now, brother," they cried to Richard, "die in the Lord, for grace has come upon you!" And then, covered in the kisses of his brothers, brother Richard was hauled to the scaffold, placed upon the guillotine and had his head lopped off in brotherly fashion, since grace had come upon him.[2]

Surely there are grounds for outrage in this story. These Christians fail to appeal for clemency for Richard on the grounds of his horrible upbringing. The class distinction is obvious: Ivan seems to imply that such eminent persons would hardly have so blithely let one of their own go to his death. And they celebrate instead Richard's spiritual conversion as evidence of God's grace, when this same God apparently cared so little for Richard as a child that God did not give him adequate food, nurture, and other necessities of a healthy upbringing.

What is also striking about Ivan's narration in the context of our current discussion, however, is Ivan's disregard precisely for an orthodox theistic angle on these events. A Christian would be dismayed, of course, at Richard's past. Nothing in Christian teaching would encourage passing over this lightly, and everything in Christian compassion would grieve over it. But a Christian would also rejoice in God's somehow working through the terrible circumstances of Richard's crime and punishment to bring him into contact with Christian people so as to result in his apparently genuine conversion. Richard is indeed, so Christians believe, now destined for eternal life—and nothing is more important, and more to be celebrated, than that.

Does Richard's conversion supposedly "make up for" his wretched life? Ivan is clear: "I declare in advance that no truth, not even the whole truth, is worth such a price."[3] The Christian might counter that the suffering of someone like Richard is not about securing "truth" in some abstract sense, but about receiving eternal life, life that vastly outweighs this one in both quality and quantity. As the apostle Paul—who had himself suffered imprisonment, torture, and ostracism—writes in the New Testament,

> This slight momentary affliction is preparing us for an eternal weight of glory beyond all measure, because we look not at what can be seen but at what cannot be seen; for what can be seen is temporary, but what cannot be seen is eternal. For we know that if the earthly tent we live in is destroyed, we have a building from God, a house not made with hands, eternal in the heavens. (II Corinthians 4:17–5:1 NRSV)

Ivan does not take seriously into account the possibility that Richard is, indeed, heading for everlasting bliss. Ivan's entire frame of reference is this world: "I want retribution, otherwise I shall destroy myself. And retribution not at some place and some time in infinity, but here upon earth, and in such a way that I see it for myself."[4] For Ivan, Richard's execution is only the last undeserved misery—made the more absurd by all this wrongheaded Christian babbling—in an unrelievedly miserable existence.

So which view of things makes sense and warrants belief? Is there a life to come? And if so, how does that life cast light upon our questions and problems in this one?

MEANS AND ENDS

Each of the main three theistic religions has a tradition of asceticism—a demanding program of physical self-denial whose purpose is to help a person concentrate on the realm of the spirit. Not only such spiritual athletes, however, but ordinary believers also must beware of excessive attachment to, and entanglement in, the good things of the world. They ought instead to set their sights on glorifying God in this life and enjoying God's blessing in the next. Self-discipline is expected of every true Jew, Christian, or Muslim. (The very word muslim means "submitted [to God].")

Self-discipline, however, is different from suffering. None of these religions affirms suffering as good in itself. Masochism is nowhere commended in the mainstream of these faiths, whatever aberrations have cropped up in each tradition. The best that can be said of suffering—and of evil more generally—is that it sometimes functions as a means toward good ends. In spite of its own irreducible malignity, evil can sometimes serve good.

Philip Yancey and Paul Brand have written helpfully about pain. Brand spent a long medical career serving patients with Hansen's disease, more widely known as leprosy. Leprosy has commonly been misunderstood as an affliction of the skin, like an extreme case of psoriasis or eczema. In fact, Hansen's disease attacks the nervous system, and particularly that part of it dedicated to relaying pain impulses. It might seem a great blessing never to experience pain again. But lepers characteristically lead a miserable existence, bruising and cutting their flesh and fracturing their bones without the normal signal of pain that damage is being done. Because unnoticed, their wounds frequently go untreated—particularly internal injuries and infections that are without outward manifestations.

Brand and Yancey conclude that, far from a curse, pain is an ingenious system of biological communication without which the quality of our lives would be seriously compromised, even fatally so.[5] This is a principle understood by every athlete recovering from an injury, and by every therapist and trainer: pain is an extraordinarily reliable guide to the pace and intensity of rehabilitation. Pain itself, then, is unpleasant: it's supposed to be, after all. And it would be well if we could do without it. But in this world, great good often comes to us from this evil.

Many of us recognize, too, that enduring hardship can produce mature character. As exertion strengthens muscle, so the difficulties of life test and improve our psyches. One cannot become patient, it seems, without being forced to wait and hope. One cannot become wise without observing life in good times and bad and thinking hard about the truths disclosed in such experiences. One cannot become compassionate without experiencing difficulty oneself and then extending sympathy to another. Each of these experiences can be evil in itself—or it may not be: exertion, waiting, hoping, and other challenges are not necessarily evil, and I don't want to argue that we somehow *need* evil in our lives to produce good character. But it seems that at least some evil experiences can occasion personal growth.

What is true for individuals can be true also for groups. Shared suffering can help build true community. Pulling together in a common crisis, setting aside petty differences in the service of a larger goal, turning one's attention from the neighbor to focus upon a larger threat—all of these aspects of coping together with a danger or disaster can form and strengthen communal ties. Such ties grow stronger with every sandbag passed from one neighbor to another as a flood threatens, with every nail hammered into a new barn after a tornado's destruction, with every bowl of soup ladled out in a shelter.

Moreover, catastrophe can severely teach us our human limitations and need. When the river spills over all of the levees we have carefully built to control it, when the lightning blazes out of the sky and sets a valley alight, when the earth shakes cities into rubble—each is an occasion to remember our finitude and our dependence. When disappointment or illness or death comes into our lives individually, it can force us to confront ultimate issues that normally lie obscured behind our everyday preoccupations.

Then again, evil in some instances might be the just outcome of evil. Some might think that reprisal, for instance, is justly provoked by malice. Waste might be justly produced by foolishness. Loneliness might be the just outcome of selfishness. And vulnerability to danger might be the just result of willful ignorance. In some instances, at least, one might plausibly consider that some evils come about as the correct and appropriate results of evil moral choices.

Finally, for believers in God, evil provides the occasion for persevering in faith. It challenges trust in God in the face of force to the contrary. And as the believer endures the evil and moves past it, her faith in God is confirmed and improved. This teaching recurs frequently in the Scriptures of Judaism, Christianity, and Islam, and many believers have testified gratefully to their experience of this principle.[6]

Yet it is also starkly clear, and must be squarely faced, that evil does not *necessarily* produce these goods. Not at all. Pain, for instance, may serve no apparent purpose. What good does it do for the terminally ill to writhe in untreatable agony in their last, wretched days and hours? Pain has nothing to tell us here that isn't obvious. Pain now is nothing but a curse. Hardship can produce stronger, deeper character, but it can also squeeze a psyche into a bitter, defensive, and anxious egotism. Disaster can build communities, but it can also tear them apart as desperate people compete for resources. Grief can remind one of ultimate questions, but it can also dispose the heart to listen to the worst possible answers.[7] Evil can justly provoke evil, but it can also provoke even worse and disproportionate evil: a driving mistake prompts a freeway murder; a misplaced joke destroys a friendship; a sloppy sentence torpedoes a diplomatic exchange. Sometimes evil can be a means to good, yes. But sometimes evil produces only more evil.

It is hardly enough, therefore, to respond to the problem of evil merely in terms of "means" and "ends," even if we should also grant that such an approach helps us understand God and evil a bit better. Sometimes evil seems only a dark, disgusting mystery. We ought to confront the possibility that there is not, and will not ever be, a humanly satisfactory explanation for this or that particular instance of evil, nor for the whole complex of evil in the world. Chapter 6 confronts this possibility and tries to offer a way in which faith in God can be rightly maintained in the face of this awful mystery. In the meantime, we can see how *some* evils might be related to *some* goods as means to ends, even as we cannot be satisfied completely with that insight.

GOD'S WILL, POWER, AND RESPONSIBILITY—AND OURS

Let us return for a moment to two axioms of classical theism (Jewish, Christian, and Muslim). Classical theism affirms that God is good: that God wills what is right and, beyond this, what is loving for God's creatures. It affirms, second, that God can perform any action that is consonant with the divine character and will.

Now, since God is a moral being, we must bear in mind the two levels of analysis we discussed under "moral evil." That is, as we try to assess God's responsibility for evil, we must attempt to judge not only

God's action (and its results), but also God's motive. And we must examine the consistency between God's express intentions and God's activity. If we assume that it is a good thing for all people to be happy all the time, for instance, and see that obviously not all people are happy all the time, then God's will appears to be deficient either in goodness (God does not want all people to be happy) or in power (God does want people to be happy, but cannot make them all so).

Let us consider this assumption. Is it truly self-evident that it is good for all people to be happy all the time? Perhaps it is not, and thus perhaps God is good not to will that all people be happy all the time. (Aldous Huxley's *Brave New World* suggests that a constant happiness induced by drugs, for instance, is not good.[8]) Suppose instead God wants every human being to become emotionally mature—say, self-controlled or sympathetic to others. And suppose that the psychology of human beings means that all people need to be unhappy at least once in order to learn from this experience something of the self-control or sympathy they need to develop.

What we are raising here in a preliminary way, the next chapter takes up directly: what is God's will? Is it good? And is it being actualized in the world? For we must consider carefully the nature of God's will before we can conclude that God is not perfectly good and all-powerful.

Before we turn to such questions about God, however, we might pause for a few moments of self-awareness. What about our will, power, and responsibility? Do we have a free will? If so, do we have power to exercise it, to bring things about that we prefer? And if this is so, must we then shoulder the responsibility for bringing those things about, including evil things?

Some ancient and modern worldviews deny that we have free will. Sociobiology and behaviorism each claim that human free will is an illusion. Our consciousness and, particularly, our conscience and will are products of the activity of the impersonal matter and energy of our brains. We are programmed, that is, and we automatically go about doing what we are programmed to do, however much we may think that we make actual choices among real alternatives.

Others do not go so far, but yet qualify our freedom. They point out that sometimes we lack the requisite intelligence or information to recognize all of the options that are before us in a given case, and so in that sense our freedom is restricted. Or perhaps we lack a healthy moral and social background out of which to make the most salutary decisions—we have less than full freedom in this case, too. All of us, lastly, live in a bewildering time in which powerful forces—especially political and economic forces—attempt to persuade us to choose what is against what we would call, in a situation of collected quiet, our better judgment. So a number of reasons qualify the idea that we have free will.

Still, in most societies, both past and present, human beings have believed that we do have free will in the sense that we are capable of making choices that are not utterly determined by some external or internal constraint. The justice system of each community, however simple or elaborate, depends upon this basic conviction that (with certain exceptions) we each are responsible for our actions.

This general trait of human society raises important issues for any confrontation with the question of God and evil. Natural evil, it seems, must be blamed on God because human beings have nothing to do with it. David Hume pictured the world as a house with problems in every room: "where the windows, doors, fires, passages, stairs, and the whole economy of the building were the source of noise, confusion, fatigue, darkness, and the extremes of heat and cold." It would be useless, Hume maintained, for God to claim that this house was the best possible—that any change would be for the worse. "Still you would assert in general, that, if the architect had had skill and good intentions [omnipotence and omnibenevolence], he might have . . . remedied all or most of these inconveniences. If you find many inconveniences and deformities in the building, you will always, without entering into any detail, condemn the architect."[9]

You might, though, blame the tenants, if they have ravaged, and continue to abuse, an originally sound structure. If an earthquake devastates a city, it seems a violent and reprehensible act of God, as Voltaire famously judged the Lisbon earthquake of 1755 to be. Yet if the city is contemporary San Francisco, and human beings continue to live near the San Andreas fault even as seismologists warn them that the Big One is likely no more than fifty years away, then when that quake comes, whose fault will the carnage and wreckage be? Who decides to cut down Amazonian rain forests, and who decides to over-till and overfertilize Iowa topsoil that slides each year into the Mississippi? Who produces pollution and gases that deplete the ozone layer, while at the same time building what some scientists believe to be a dangerous "greenhouse" in the atmosphere? Our evil backgrounds and current environments that "make" us or "help" us toward evil— again, how much ought to be traced to human responsibility?

Cornelius Plantinga points to the reality of our complicity in so-called natural evils:

> Thousands of Third World children die daily from largely preventable diseases: out of laziness or complacency, certain grownups fail to prevent them. Thousands of First World children are born drug addicts: their mothers have hooked them in the womb. Some people with sexually transmitted diseases knowingly put new partners at terrible risk. It happens every day.[10]

Furthermore, *whatever* we are given as our lot in life—whether from genetics or Mother's behavior while we are in the womb or family relationships or neighborhood environment—we are responsible for what we do with what we have. As Plantinga observes, "Nobody is more insistent than A.A. [Alcoholics Anonymous] that alcoholism is a disease; nobody is more insistent than A.A. on the need for the alcoholic to take full responsibility for his disease and to deal with it in brutal candour."[11] We recognize both evils "out there" in nature and evils "in here" that may well be rooted in our physicality. Yet however much we can rightly blame others, even God, for the presence of such evils, we are responsible to deal with them as morally as we can.

Let's grant, then, the reality of human agency in a variety of instances of so-called natural evil. Don't we then want God to unmake the negative consequences of these actions? Why doesn't God step in to save us, we might ask, even from ourselves? But let us consider what we are asking here. If God does so step in, such continual inter-vention has implications for human dignity, for the order of the world, and perhaps for the ultimate good of human life. Maybe, in fact, it is *best* that God *does not* intervene, and lets us both make choices and live with the consequences.

Before we leave this theme, however, let us recognize simply this: an informed and mature human response to evil will include taking responsibility for our share in it. When a reporter asked Mother Teresa, "Where is God?" when a baby dies alone in a Calcuttan alley, she offered this much-quoted response. "God is there, suffering with that baby," she said. "The question really is, where are *you*?"

CHAPTER FIVE

A Good World After All?

PHILOSOPHERS HAVE DEBATED FOR CENTURIES whether this is the "best of all possible worlds." Note that they have not debated whether this is the best of all *imaginable* worlds, for we all can imagine (or at least we think we can imagine) a world that improves on this one. The philosophical debate instead attempts to decide whether, given all the factors involved, this world is in fact the best of all possible options.

We might first consider, however, whether this world is a *good* world, let alone the "best possible." Some contemporary philosophers have argued that the problem of God and evil is adequately resolved if we can conclude that the world is, on the whole, a good world, rather than the best possible. Some say this because they believe that God is not logically obliged to create the best possible world, but just a good one. Others say this because they believe that the concept of "best possible world" is problematic, even incapable of formulation: for example, if a good world is G, then a better world would be G plus an additional good yielding G + 1, and so on infinitely.[1] So let us content ourselves, at least for the moment, with what seems more than enough work: to decide whether the world is actually good.

THE POINT OF IT ALL

Usually we intend this expression to denote the purpose, or the meaning, of something. But another word in English, "end," conveys even better the double sense of the word "point" in this context. For "the end of it all" would suggest both the termination (so "end-point") and the purpose (the point), of all that we experience. When philosophers (who habitually use this second meaning of "end") ask, "What is the end of something?" they are asking not just how it finishes, but what it exists for, what it finally is to achieve. Judaism, Christianity, and Islam share the conviction that all of history is moving toward a final consummation that will make plain the true meaning of all things. Therefore, they affirm, the present is best understood by reference to the future.

What is that future? All three faiths affirm that the ultimate end—both the purpose and the final state—of human life is to live in peace with God and with our fellow creatures. This peace is much more than the mere absence of conflict. Instead, I mean what the ancient Hebrews meant by *shalom*: a full-orbed, comprehensive, and harmonious wholesomeness in each particular creature, in the relationships among creatures, and in their relationships with God. Thus shalom is an entire cosmos of goodness: natural, human, angelic, and divine. Note that the end is not mere human happiness. God could, one supposes, simply alter our mental states for eternity and let us "bliss out" in an endless and mindless euphoria. But this is not a vision of fulfilled human life. It is a degraded, selfish, subhuman existence. Nor is the end of creation just comfort, or freedom, or health, or prosperity. These things, good in themselves, are all just glimpses of the global goodness God intends for creation in which each part is itself complete and nicely plays its role in the joyful and fruitful society of peace.[2]

Now for us to be fit to participate in this ultimate world, two realities must be faced. First, as individuals and as communities, we are in a negative condition: we are not peaceful. We are corrupt, weak, mean, unstable, and destructive of shalom.[3] In our hearts and in our relationships we are far from whole. And we have been so throughout our history. Judaism, Christianity, and Islam call this condition sin, and they say that sin must be faced and dealt with.

Second, if we could be healed of this pathology, we would still need to positively grow up into spiritual adulthood. We must mature in love, in dedication, in purity, in joy, in faithfulness, in enthusiasm, in patience, and in a host of other virtues. We are not all bad: we know enough to recognize something of the meaning of each of these terms, and we are good enough to practice these virtues from time to time. But our customary excuses—"I'm not as bad as he is," or "Hey, I haven't killed anybody!" or "I mean well," or "Nobody's perfect," or "Everybody does it"—sound distastefully inadequate at the gate of God's divine garden, at the door of God's splendid city of light. (As C. S. Lewis has pointed out, such excuses also are entirely inadequate to deal with our problems here and now. We cannot possibly live together and heal the earth as long as we keep underestimating the enormity of our evil.[4]) No, to take our proper places in God's shalom will mean both healing from our negative condition and growth into spiritual maturity. Then—but only then—can we enjoy everlasting life with God and each other.

THE FREE WILL DEFENSE

One of the most trenchant philosophical responses of our time to the question of God and evil has been advanced by Alvin Plantinga, in the company of like-minded others. In the so-called Free Will Defense, Plantinga answers particularly a classic essay by J. L. Mackie that asserts that theists cannot simultaneously affirm three propositions: that God is good, that God is all-powerful, and that evil exists. The theist simply must compromise, or give up outright, one of these three affirmations. To round out his argument, Mackie specifies additional premises: "that good is opposed to evil, in such a way that a good thing always eliminates evil as far as it can, and that there are no limits to what an omnipotent thing can do."[5] Plantinga's response is complicated, requiring dozens of pages to lay out even in the dense style of analytical philosophy. But in essence it goes like this:[6]

God desired to love and be loved by other beings. God created human beings with this in view. To make us capable of such fellowship, God had to give us the freedom to choose, because love, though it does have its elements of "compulsion," is meaningful only when it is neither automatic nor coerced. This sort of free will, however, entailed the danger that it would be used *not* to enjoy God's love and to love God in return, but to go one's own way in defiance of both God and one's own best interest. This is what the story of Adam and Eve in the Garden of Eden portrays.

It is important to note that nothing in this conception of free will makes it *necessary* for human beings to choose evil. Free will in this sense just means an authentic possibility. A human being in this condition could, theoretically, always make good choices and never choose evil in perfect freedom. There is nothing inescapably or essentially human about sinning! Only the *possibility* of sin is intrinsic to this idea of human free will.

I have added qualifiers to the expressions for "free will" in the two previous paragraphs (such as "free will *in this sense*") because there are different kinds of free will. We must understand Adam and Eve to have been created in a state of innocence, not in a state of moral perfection. The former means that they started with a clean slate, with no disposition to do wrong. They could, however, choose evil at any moment. The latter means something quite different—a point not always recognized in this sort of discussion. Moral perfection, as opposed to mere innocence, means complete moral maturity, a character of holiness confirmed through a lifetime of moral choices. It is such a state of moral perfection that Christians believe they will enjoy one day in heaven. They will not have lost free will (they are still free to do what they prefer), but they will be so thoroughly habituated in goodness that they simply will not sin. We see an approximation of this condition in our current circumstances: a devoted mother would never torture her child, nor an ardent patriot ever betray his country for a dollar. These people are in one sense truly free to commit such actions, but we would say that it is *morally impossible* for them to do so, given their convictions. Yet we would still recognize that their wills are free. So Adam and Eve had free will, but of a different sort. As new beings, Adam and Eve did not possess mature moral character. Adam and Eve started out innocent, not perfect.

(I will take up the story of Adam and Eve again. There is, of course, serious question as to how literally to understand the existence of these two figures. For our present purposes, however, we can leave this aside and simply note that they stand for "how human beings started out.")

Now, for God to grant human beings free will was to grant us the awful dignity of making real choices with real consequences. Were God to compel us to make only good choices, then we would not be making choices at all, but merely following God's directions as a computer executes a program. Were God to allow us to make choices but then constantly intervene to prevent anything bad from resulting from those choices, like a parent constantly interfering in a baby's play to keep it from harm, it is difficult to see how those choices would have integrity and significance. Some Christian philosophers have asserted in this regard that if we were always prevented from performing truly evil actions, then we would not have free will. In this sense, they argue, the existence of gratuitous evils does not militate against belief in God after all, but rather confirms the free will defense's claim that we really do have freedom to choose good or evil.[7] I suggest that even if every one of our negative choices was instantly rectified by divine intervention, we might still will to do evil, and this willing would itself be genuine evil action (such as the murderous fantasizing of someone who doesn't ever commit an actual homicide). Still, if God kept preventing anything bad from resulting from our choices, it is not clear what "freedom" would mean in such a context, nor is it obvious what important truth we would learn about ourselves in such an insulated world.

Moreover, as we already discussed under "means and ends," sometimes the evil done by one agent results, in God's providence, in good for another—or even for the perpetrator himself. One might think of the Biblical story of Joseph, who is sold into slavery by his brothers. This is an evil action that ultimately led to Joseph's being appointed the pharaoh's deputy in Egypt and thus enabled to save those brothers and their families from famine: "Even though you intended to do harm to me," Joseph later would tell them, "God intended it for good" (Genesis 50:20). It is not clear, then, that it really would be best for God to eradicate every consequence of evil intentions and actions, because evil can sometimes have, in God's kind irony, good effects.

We must consider carefully, perhaps more carefully than we normally do, just what we are asking when we wish God would destroy the evil in the world. God could do so, after all, by a worldwide cataclysm that would wipe the slate clean. But wouldn't that entail such evils as the mass destruction of innocent children, animals, and plants? (The strange Biblical tale of Noah's ark implies, but never answers, this question.) Perhaps God could simply wipe out all the bad human beings and leave the good ones behind. But who among us then would fit in each category? I myself certainly am not entirely good, and a perfect God would have to apply a perfect standard. Such a standard would entail my own eradication, and that of my family and friends. Are you and your loved ones up to that test?

Perhaps God could make us stop sinning somehow, and ultimately rid the world of natural evils, too. Let us now take up the former question of moral evil again. If God made us stop sinning by somehow forcing goodness upon us and thus compromising the freedom of our wills, then we and God both would lose the goodness of authentic love, among other goods. But if instead God caused us to outgrow sin and grow up into goodness, then nothing good would be lost (although much might have to be endured), and much good would be gained. And that, as I shall argue, is what God in fact is doing.

Perhaps, however, God could have looked ahead and discovered (if that is the right word) which possible human beings would sin and which would choose well, and then actualize only the latter human beings. God thus would not have compromised human freedom, but would also have allowed no evil to result from it.[8]

Mackie himself raises this cogent objection. Plantinga suggests in response that perhaps we human beings suffer from a condition he calls "transworld depravity," a condition in which no matter what the circumstances, each of us will commit at least one sin, and maybe many. We do so, that is, because it is somehow in our essence, or nature, to do so. If God, for some reason (perhaps known only to God) wants to enjoy the fellowship of these particular beings, then God is perfectly just in creating us and letting us loose, as it were, to be who we are, sin and all.

Suppose that part of my essence is to be greedy, and such a trait, of course, shapes much of my personality. If God creates me minus my avarice, the resulting person is "better," but it is not *me*. If God prefers to create me and not someone else, God must actualize all of me, including my avarice. God's omnipotence is not compromised in this case: God can work only with what is logically possible, and creating me minus my greediness is logically impossible.

Plantinga does not say that he personally believes that all of us human beings do, in fact, suffer from transworld depravity. He simply suggests, for the sake of his argument with Mackie and others, that transworld depravity is possible. Indeed, Plantinga goes so far as to say that *all* human beings—even potential ones—may suffer from transworld depravity. If this were so, he concludes, even an omnipotent God could not create human beings that wouldn't commit at least one evil. God therefore could not avoid evil by the simple expedient of creating people other than ourselves if somehow all other possible people also suffer from transworld depravity.

Why then does God put up with all the evil wrought by generations of human beings through the ages? God does so, Plantinga and others argue, because *on the whole* it is for the best—or, at least, for the better. God, to put it bluntly, calculates the "cost-benefit ratio" and deems the cost of evil to be worth the benefit of loving and enjoying the love of these human beings.

(It is crucial to underline that *love* is the highest good that God seeks in this enterprise, not *freedom* per se. Much philosophy of religion seems to me to have gone astray on this point by arguing over whether or not freedom is worth all the evil entailed in our world. But freedom is a kind of instrumental good in the theistic scheme, not a final good in itself. In this case, freedom is simply a requirement of the higher good of love—and *that* might indeed be worth it all.)

Furthermore, Plantinga & Co. continue, to argue that God is doing a bad job of running the world in terms of the ratio of evil to good is more problematic than some people assume. How can such people be so sure that alleviating or preventing a particular evil can be accomplished without the loss of some accompanying good? How do they *know* that this minor problem, or that major evil, is just a mistake or just a tragedy or just an absurdity whose positive consequences do not outweigh its negative ones? (In this same light, how can such critics so confidently claim that God does *not* in fact occasionally suspend the laws of nature to prevent the evil that would otherwise occur—occasionally, to be sure, so that the benefits to us of living in a regulated universe are not compromised? I am not saying that God does do so—although Biblical and more recent accounts of miracles do attest to such events. In the spirit of the Free Will Defense, I am simply putting the burden of proof back on the critics to show that such things definitely do not happen.)

So, the Free Will Defense concludes, theists *can* simultaneously affirm that God is good, that God is all-powerful, and that evil yet exists. It is important to remember that Mackie's charge of inconsistency is an absolute one: the theist can in *no way* consistently hold belief in God's power, goodness, and the existence of evil. All Plantinga has to do for an adequate philosophical defense is to show that theists can do so in *at least one* way. The consensus among philosophers of religion (and consensus doesn't emerge easily among this crowd) is that Plantinga has done this successfully.

Still, the Free Will Defense is just that: a defense. It is not a positive statement of what Alvin Plantinga or anyone else really thinks is the way God manages the world. Furthermore, it does not deal with the huge category of natural evil, except in a surprisingly offhand way. In a very short section, Plantinga simply wonders whether natural disasters are the result of the work of demons, which would make natural evil a subcategory of moral evil. So one well might wonder whether more than a defense can be offered. Can theists do more than just repel the attack of an "atheologian" like Mackie and actually set out a positive case?

Such positive explanations, such attempts to describe God's ways to human beings in philosophical or theological terms, are called *theodicies*. Perhaps the Free Will Defense can point toward a Free Will Theodicy.

A FREE WILL THEODICY

Let us now set out clearly three propositions of theistic belief that can be derived from our explorations so far. First, God created the world and continues to sustain it. Nothing happens, therefore, that God does not allow and, in at least a fundamental way, enable to happen. God is—and we must face this squarely—in an ultimate sense responsible for everything that happens, since God allows it, even if God does not act to make it happen. God is responsible for everything that exists, since God created and sustains it. This proposition is nothing other than the express teaching of the Jewish, Christian, and Muslim Scriptures. Each of them, in fact, records God making a declaration like the following, which appears in one of the greatest of Jewish prophecies: "I form light and create darkness, I make weal and create woe; I the LORD do all these things" (Isaiah 45:7). In this ultimate sense, as Christian theologian Henri Blocher affirms, "God 'wills' evil, he decides that evil shall occur."[9]

This assertion makes many theists profoundly uncomfortable. Some bob and weave around the idea, hoping to blame human free will or demonic power or some intrinsic flaw in the universe for evil, so as to exonerate God. Some take the tack of Harold Kushner in his bestseller, *When Bad Things Happen to Good People*, as he champions God's goodness at the expense of God's power. For such theists, God means well and deeply sympathizes with those who suffer, but God is not capable of governing the world so as to prevent all evil. Evil occurs, that is, despite God's preference for good.[10]

Either or both of these alternative views may be right. But they give rise to their own problems. Both of them see the universe as containing evil places and persons that remain beyond God's sovereign influence; God cannot either defeat or redeem those places and persons. Such a limited God therefore cannot guarantee the ultimate and comprehensive destruction of evil and the ultimate and comprehensive victory of good. Such views, in short, preserve God's reputation for moral goodness, but deeply compromise the classic theistic hope for a perfectly good future brought about by God's supreme power. (I frankly don't understand why proponents of such views don't worry more about this.) So let's return to the traditional view of God, a view that *does* offer this hope, and see how persuasive it is in light of the problem of evil.

The second proposition of classic theistic belief on our list is that God created human beings with the capacity to make real moral choices. God preferred to create, and work with, and care for, and enjoy the company of human beings who would have the power to choose to return love to God and love their fellow creatures, or to turn against God and mistreat others. God preferred the good that would come from a relationship with these free beings—even taking into consideration the evils that would also result—over creating automatons that never did wrong but also were, by definition, incapable of love.

Third, human beings chose once, and have chosen many times since, to defy God's guidance and blessing and to prefer their own wisdom and provision. And these many, many choices have had global and cumulative effects: universal human alienation, confusion, and destruction, which have also affected much of the natural world in the forms of pollution, exploitation, and so on. Cornelius Plantinga considers a single case study of terrible psychological illness described by psychiatrist Scott Peck, and then muses:

> That's just one patient. Let him and his kin, plus ordinary sinners and pretty good persons and everybody else, sow and reap and sow again; let them fertilize and cross-fertilize each other, and the resulting culture will defy rational analysis.[11]

Christian theologians have wrangled for centuries over the idea of original sin. Without getting too deeply into this debate, we can all observe the obvious: no one starts with a clean slate. We all inherit dispositions from our ancestors, and some of those traits are evil. We all grow up in families that shape us, and some of that shaping is evil. We all live within social structures that encourage certain attitudes and behaviors, and many of them are evil. And we all, each of us, without exception, commit evil—even according to our own moral standards, let alone according to those of a perfect Deity. So however sin originated in us as individuals or in the world at large, here it is, within and without, and we have to respond to it as best we can.

I would echo the assertion of Henri Blocher that the Bible simply does not explain why Adam and Eve sinned, and gives few hints as to why God allowed them to do so.[12] The Bible just asserts that they did. Alvin Plantinga's hypothesis of "transworld depravity" may work as a logical defense in the realm of analytical philosophy (and that is all Plantinga intends to accomplish thereby). But Christian (or Jewish or Muslim) theology presents no reason to believe that human beings do *necessarily* commit at least one sin. To speak more precisely, human beings *since the Fall of Adam and Eve* might well all have some intrinsic flaw that disposes us toward sin. This universal flaw, whatever it is, is what is customarily meant by "original sin." But the flaw is just that: a departure from the original design of human beings in moral innocence. If we wind the clock back to the original human beings *before* their first sin, then we might well wonder with J. L. Mackie and other critics why God allowed the drama of sin to unfold.

It is one thing to hold, therefore, that transworld depravity is possible. It is another thing to believe that it is even likely to be true. To put forward transworld depravity as more than a logical possibility seems odd indeed: cannot or would not God create human beings without such a flaw? Such an idea seems simply to push the problem of evil back one step to the question of why a good and omnipotent and omniscient God cannot or would not prevent evil from occurring by preventing the existence of beings who would commit evil, and creating others that would freely do only good.

Philosopher William Hasker raises an interesting point about *our*

situation, about how we feel about God and evil in the present cir-
cumstance of living in a world that is thoroughly infected by evil, and
this point bears on the issue of God's responsibility for the origin of
evil. Hasker suggests that (a) if I do not regret my own existence nor
(b) the existence of those whom I love, and (c) if my own existence
and the existence of those I love depends on the previous existence of
a long line of ancestors, all of whom sinned, plus (d) a global history
of troubles that doubtless influenced my family tree and the ancestry
of those I love, then I cannot condemn God outright for allowing
any evil, or even a lot of evil, in God's administration of the world. I
cannot do so, Hasker asserts, because at least *some* evil in the past—
indeed, probably much evil—was instrumental in making it possible
for me and my loved ones to be born, and I don't regret those events.
Therefore I must conclude that *on the whole* I prefer the world, evils and
all, to some possible world with fewer evils that nonetheless would
have resulted in the nonexistence of myself or those I love.[13]

Peter Kreeft proffers a similar argument. He contends that each of
us, day by day, must be making the judgment that *on the whole* life is
worth all of the evils it contains. For, as Kreeft provocatively puts it,

> You haven't committed suicide. You've decided, for whatever
> reason, or even for no reason, to live. . . . In the middle of the
> story that is your life, are you glad you're in it? You've
> answered yes by choosing to stay alive. You must believe you
> have more pluses than minuses in your life, because you
> could always move to zero, but you don't.[14]

Kreeft, I think, overstates things a bit. Many people refuse to commit suicide because they are afraid of what would happen to loved
ones who survived them, or to themselves on the unknown further
shores of death—not because they are "glad" to be alive. Still, Kreeft's
main point remains: most of us do accept life on the whole, tough as
it is, as preferable to the drastic alternative of death. And this decision,
he argues, is analogous to God's preferring the benefits of the continued existence of this world, troubles and all, to extinguishing it.

Whether or not one agrees with these arguments, they do raise an important consideration in an intriguing way. Maybe God preferred and continues to prefer the cost of evil in the world to the cost of never actualizing the particular human beings (like you and me) who would, in some respects, result from (and contribute to) that evil. And maybe, from my own much more limited perspective, I would agree: I would rather there be this world, with me and my loved ones in it, than some other world in which I and my loved ones didn't exist. Such musings do not resolve the *logical* question of God and evil, as Hasker himself notes, and they certainly are not compelling arguments. But they challenge us to consider that perhaps God would not be wrong to make a similar choice on a global scale.

Another consideration, respecting the limitation of our intellects, also deserves our attention. Could our attempt to figure out how evil can "make sense" in a theistic, and particularly Christian, scheme of things be itself a wrongheaded project? Could the very mysteriousness and absurdity of evil, its very lack of "fit" in our cosmos, point to its nonessential and temporary nature? Could the difficulty that the best minds have had in trying to find a place for evil in the great scheme of things be explained by the basic theistic conviction that *evil has no place in the great scheme of things, except to be destroyed?* We do well to pause over this possibility.

Yet what does this thought do to the idea that the global "cost: benefit" ratio works out better with the evil we have in the world than if no evil had occurred? On the one hand, if evil has no permanent place in the great scheme of things, then God's providence as we currently experience it is, so to speak, God making the best of a bad situation that came about contrary to God's own preference. On the other hand, if God intended all along not only to run the risk of free human beings sinning, but to allow things actually to take this course with full foreknowledge of the consequences—and did so because God preferred *on the whole* the global result of the drama of sin and salvation to a world without it—then it rather sounds as if evil was *necessary* for that drama and thus evil *does* have a place in the great scheme of things.

Perhaps these two ideas are not as contradictory as they appear, however. God originally created the universe entirely good, yet with the potential for evil to enter through the free agents God created. Evil had no place in such a cosmos. When evil began, however, as God foreknew it would, greater good resulted out of the subsequent events than would have resulted had God created a universe with less evil, or no sin at all, or different beings, or whatever. And, as theists believe, the ultimate destiny of the world God did create is to be restored to a situation without evil, for evil can have no *lasting* place in God's creation. However it functions instrumentally in God's providence, therefore, evil is fundamentally anomalous and temporary. It cannot survive in the ultimate state of God's cosmos.

Let us return from this speculation (for that is all it is) about God's plan for the universe and consider God's concern for us as human beings. If these three main propositions are true—that God creates and sustains the world; that God created human beings with moral freedom; and that human beings have misused that freedom to sin—then a good world would be one in which two kinds of problems were dealt with: our starting from "less than zero" and our need to grow to maturity.[15]

First, a good world would teach us about sin and evil: it would describe our negative situation. It would show us at least something of the magnitude of our deviation from God's goodwill and the extent of the deadly consequences of our sin. It would demonstrate our limitations and our defects, and thus something of our great need for forgiveness and rehabilitation. And it would do so in the face of our proud denial that anything is really, permanently wrong with us that science and technology and goodwill cannot soon take care of. Cultural critic Neil Postman sharpens this point in his depiction of our culture as a "Technopoly," a city of mere technique:

> In Technopoly, all experts are invested with the charisma of priestliness. Some of our priest-experts are called psychiatrists, some psychologists, some sociologists, some statisticians. The god they serve does not speak of righteousness or goodness or mercy or grace. Their god speaks of efficiency, precision, objectivity. And that is why such concepts as sin

and evil disappear in Technopoly. They come from a moral universe that is irrelevant to the theology of expertise. And so the priests of Technopoly call sin "social deviance," which is a statistical concept, and they call evil "psychopathology," which is a medical concept. Sin and evil disappear because they cannot be measured and objectified, and therefore cannot be dealt with by experts.[16]

Cornelius Plantinga recently wrote an entire book on sin in order

to renew the knowledge of a persistent reality that used to evoke in us fear, hatred, and grief. Many of us have lost this knowledge, and we ought to regret the loss. For slippage in our consciousness of sin, like most fashionable follies, may be pleasant, but it is also devastating. Self-deception about our sin is a narcotic, a tranquilizing and disorienting suppression of our spiritual central nervous system.

Plantinga changes metaphors: sin makes us "religiously . . . unmusical. . . . Moral beauty begins to bore us. The idea that the human race needs a Savior sounds quaint."[17]

A good world would also tell us, however, that we are not merely loathsome evil creatures, a verdict that would spell our doom. Instead, a good world would assure us of the astonishing truth that we are creatures whom God still loves, who are capable of being restored, and who could again be beautiful and strong and noble. It would give us hope that rescue is possible and, indeed, available—that there is a Savior who meets our need for forgiveness and healing.

Second, a good world would provide opportunities for personal growth that would help us go beyond the eradication of our faults to mature in love for God and for each other. It would, as Cornelius Plantinga says, help us to "cultivate a taste for this project [of shalom], to become more and more the sort of person for whom eternal life with God would be sheer heaven."[18] A good world would be a kind of boot camp or training center—an obstacle course, and encounter group, and extended family, and pilgrim community all at once. It would challenge us every day, from every angle, to grow up—and would do so without allowing us to be so crushed by evil that we could not possibly complete the regimen. As in the case of suffering Job, God restrains evil (whether Satan or some other instigator) so as not to defeat God's ultimate purposes, not to press us beyond our capacities. As Martin Luther wrote,

> The power of the devil is not as great as it appears to be out-wardly; for if he had full power to rage as he pleased, you would not live for one hour or retain safe and intact a single sheep, a crop in the field, corn in the barn, and, in short, any of those things which pertain to this life. . . . To be sure, he causes disturbance, and yet he is not able to carry out what he most desires, to overthrow all things.[19]

What then do we find in our world? We find the world to be an arena in which God reaches out in love to estranged and damaged creatures and helps them mature into reconciled relationships with each other. Thus we live in a world in which human beings clearly have at least a measure of free will to do both good and evil, and to live with the consequences of their choices. We find ourselves in a world in which we can see the terrible results of human sin as well as the salutary results of human obedience to God and love for one's neighbor. The world holds up to us a mirror that is daunting to con-template.

It is not a perfect mirror. Indeed, in many places the world is a distorting mirror that seems to say that virtue is foolish and vice is shrewd. Of course, in a world whose systems are so infected by sin, we ought to expect that sometimes evil will succeed. But even then, a deeper order often prevails, and justice is done. We glimpse the tem-porariness and artificiality of systems that reward evil, and we sense the permanence of true justice, however elusive it seems to be now.

Second, we find our world to be one that offers many opportuni-ties to learn about and to do good. Others are in need, whether because of their own choices, or those of others, or because of natural evil. Their need beckons to us, and we respond—somehow. For whether we turn away, or vacillate, or defer a decision, each is a significant ethical response. We live in a world in which suffering, whether our own or others', challenges us to go beyond our current state of personal development to greater moral virtue, whether courage, perseverance, generosity, or hope.

Surely, however, it is one thing for someone to contract lung cancer after a lifetime of smoking in defiance of the danger. It is quite another thing for someone to contract a disease such as muscular dystrophy or multiple sclerosis (MS) that has no basis in any moral decision he or she made. How can such a personal disaster have any place in a good world?

First, we must be careful not to underestimate, as many do, the extremity of our situation and thus the extremity of the means necessary for our restoration. Perhaps forty years of disease is precisely what an individual needs to make his or her way toward the goal of eternal wholeness. To say this, I grant, seems callous, even monstrous. What a terrible thing to imply about a person's spiritual condition! And I do want to suggest another way to look at this in a moment.

But for now, let's realize that whether to tell the truth about our actual condition is the same issue that confronts an oncologist looking at grim test results. It is more "pleasant" for the physician to lie about the illness, saying that it is less serious than it is. Told such a well-meant lie, the patient can continue for a while with a happier frame of mind: "I'm not so sick after all." But health matters more than happiness. Indeed, the physician realizes that the patient's long-term happiness depends on his health, and thus requires the short-term unhappiness of dealing squarely with his current illness. Moreover, for the physician to mislead the patient—even if the patient would prefer to be misled—is malpractice. The doctor has a duty to tell the truth and to prescribe just what is needed, no matter how unpleasant, to deal with the medical reality. The cancer is virulent and tough, so the treatment must be extreme. Bad news, yes. But true news.

What is even worse, in our case, is that evil has addled our minds, not just infected our bodies. We can't think straight about it. We're delusional: "I'm not that bad, not that sick, not that needy." Or perhaps we think, as our pain rages, "No good can possibly be worth this suffering. Just let me alone." Nor would we have the courage to confront and endure, if it visibly stretched out before us year upon year, what would be necessary to restore us to health. In order to give us every opportunity for ultimate blessing, therefore, God must intervene and commit us to a regimen of rehabilitation that we do not and would not choose.

Nicholas Wolterstorff lost his twenty-five-year-old son in a mountaineering accident. He can speak from experience that I, thank God, cannot. Weeks afterward, he wrote that he had been deeply changed by the tragedy, changed for the better. But Wolterstorff also spoke honestly for those who grieve when he cried, "Without a moment's hesitation I would exchange those changes for Eric back." We would not have the fortitude to choose this path, even if we knew it to be for our good. It would be simply too terrible. God as a wise parent, though, gives us what we need, not what we think we want—even as God, as a loving parent, mourns every tear we must shed in the process.[20]

Second, I reflect on the fact that my own grandmother had MS for decades. Yet she did not seem to need such a terrible pressure on a soul that was, from my viewpoint at least, already sweet and strong. It seems quite unlikely to me that my grandmother's spiritual state required the regimen of this much suffering. My grandfather, however, has testified with tears that having to retire before his time and care for my grandmother for two decades before her eventual death changed him a great deal, and entirely for the better. Moreover, the rest of the family has noticed the positive change and are themselves different because of it—in ever-widening circles of influence that, Christians believe, make a difference for eternity. Furthermore, if we consider things from my grandmother's side, those of us who knew her could well believe her capable of choosing to endure great suffering if it meant much lasting blessing for her beloved husband and family, had God given her the choice.[21]

We must beware, then, of assuming that some people suffer more than others because they themselves need more extensive therapy than others. This is "blaming the victim" of an especially pernicious variety. It may be instead that God entrusts certain kinds of suffering only to those with the souls to bear it, and particularly suffering for the benefit of people around them.[22] I don't know why my beautiful grandmother had to suffer so much and for so long. But I can see some possible, even likely, explanations that help me believe that Grandma did not suffer for nothing, but instead for lasting, even eternal, good.[23]

Such is the experience of us all: life offers us chances to grow up. Some of us don't take them or misuse them, sadly, and we remain "stuck." We all know adults who seem permanently immature. Some even decline in character as they move from an honest ambivalence in early years toward a confirmed habit of evil, decision by decision, step by step. We also, if we are blessed, know people who continue to ripen into old age, demonstrating a nobility of soul that only increases as the years take their toll on physical health.

We also can recognize that God provides the resources necessary to meet these challenges. God provides companionship in the Holy Spirit in people's hearts, and also through the company of other believers and questers. God provides information through the Bible and in the wisdom of sages across the world. God provides protection from evil forces—natural, human, and demonic—sometimes dramatically, and always at least enough so that they do not overwhelm us and cause us to despair in spite of ourselves. Even in circumstances that an onlooker would deem dreadful—and sometimes especially in privation and suffering—God provides peace and joy, as many have testified. Sometimes, alternatively, God provides strength just enough to hang on—to life, to faith. But God provides what is needed in the light of "the point of it all," to bring us to full maturity.

As Brian Gerrish puts it,

> Suffering becomes bearable insofar as Christians recognize in it not an inflexible divine will that no one can resist, but the hand of the best of fathers, who is providing for their salva-

tion in the very act of laying a cross upon them. This is the difference between philosophical and Christian patience. It makes it possible for afflictions to be borne with a quiet, thankful mind, even a cheerful heart.[24]

What I am suggesting—and only suggesting, not "proving" or "concluding"—is that our world seems remarkably suited in many ways precisely to the needs that classical theism says we have. It is not, as some religions and philosophies assert, a world merely to escape, or to exploit, or to endure. It is a world to enjoy and be educated by. It is a world to engage and embrace. It is a world that, damaged as it is, will do us sick people good if we see it clearly and live in it wisely.

Is this a full-blown theodicy, a comprehensive explanation of how and why God runs the world as God does? No, it obviously isn't. In particular, it does not explain why God would permit this or that particular instance of evil. But these reflections offer one way to extend the Free Will Defense a little further, to consider that perhaps, after all, some good sense can be made of our general condition, of the world as we have it, and of the teachings of Judaism, Christianity, and Islam about it all.

CHAPTER SIX

The Fork in the Road

I THINK IT IS OBVIOUS THAT THE ARGUMENTS offered here so far do not provide a fully satisfactory response to the question of God and evil. Lest anyone be too easily content with such a theodicy, or any theodicy, let us come back down to earth via the words of Ivan Karamazov—Fyodor Dostoyevsky's fictional antagonist of all easy Christian thinking, and particularly of theodicy:

> [Some] progressively educated parents subjected [their] poor five-year-old girl to every torture one could think of. They beat her, flogged her, kicked her, themselves not knowing why, turned her whole body into a mass of bruises; at last they attained the highest degree of refinement: in the cold and freezing weather they locked her up for a whole night in the outside latrine because she did not ask to be relieved (as though a five-year-old child, sleeping its sound, angelic sleep, could learn to ask to be relieved at such an age)—what is more, they smeared her eyes, cheeks and mouth all over with faeces and compelled her to eat those faeces, and it was the mother, the mother who did the compelling! And that

mother was able to sleep hearing at night the moans of the poor little child, locked up in the foul latrine! So now do you understand, when a small creature that is not yet able to make sense of what is happening to it beats its hysterical breast in a foul latrine, in the dark and cold, with its tiny fist and wails with its bloody, meek, rancourless tears to "dear Father God" to protect it—now do you understand all that rot [of theodicy]?[1]

Even if the arguments I have offered to this point succeed in all they attempt (and each reader, of course, will decide that for himself or herself), the most they can do is two things: first, to indicate that there are a number of important issues involved in any intelligent attempt to wrestle with this question; and second, to show that there are some plausible ways to view those issues that make it *less difficult* to believe that God is entirely good and all-powerful in spite of evil. The answers offered so far may be true, but even so, they are not adequate.[2]

For the world *has* so much evil in it. So much, in fact, that many of us, like Ivan Karamazov, are tempted to lose faith in the goodness and power of God, or never to develop that faith in the first place. We are tempted to abandon the very idea of God, or to settle for a compromise God of limited goodness or power or both. Furthermore, we live in a world in which there is so much evil that we are tempted to abandon the effort to love our neighbor, whether our human associates or the other beings with whom we share this planet.

The nineteenth-century German philosopher Friedrich Nietzsche—virulent anti-Christian that he was—saw many things clearly and put them sharply. Nietzsche drew a stark conclusion from the eclipse of strong, vital faith in God, the eclipse whose shadow was passing over most of Europe in his day. Nietzsche asserted that the strongest human beings not only will triumph, but *ought to triumph*, over all others, and exploit them for their own purposes. For there was no overarching reason, no divinely given morality, no Absolute Lawgiver to say otherwise. Nietzsche's ideal Supermen were not, as they are sometimes caricatured by his critics, mere brutes and thugs.

Nietzsche's own heroes were such figures as Goethe and Napoleon and Wagner, and he assuredly did not look forward to the triumph of such barbarians as the Nazis. But his grasp of the moral situation without God was sure. This world is such a moral chaos that unless there is a God to explain and order and ultimately rehabilitate it, human beings with sufficient power can impose their own order and desires upon it.

Why, then, ought theists to continue to disagree with seers like Nietzsche—or even ordinary folk like us, who perhaps have real trouble, even desperate trouble, believing in God in the face of evil? Are there any more substantial grounds upon which to base one's faith?

I believe there are. But I believe that we now encounter a basic choice. If God wants to be understood by us as all-good and all-powerful, then God has but two options. The first is this: God can explain divine ways to us: not only generally (so explaining "evil" in general) but also in every particular instance that concerns us (as in "Why did I lose that job?" and "Why is my child sick?" and "Why is there still war all over Africa?"). God must offer us, that is, a complete theodicy.

A COMPLETE THEODICY

A complete theodicy would consist of a complete account of all the evil we encounter, both natural and moral, past and present, general and particular. However God would do it (a voice in our heads? a visual display? an angel?), God would explain everything to us at every turn so that we had not a flicker of doubt, not a moment's worry, that God might not be entirely good or all-powerful. Wouldn't this be terrific? No more asking, "Why?" and having no answer. A completely satisfying answer would be rendered on demand.

Many Christians (and perhaps this is true among Jews and Muslims as well) happily entertain what is, as far as I can see, the ecclesiastical equivalent of an urban myth. This church myth is widespread, but seems utterly groundless in the Scriptures. And the myth is this: "Someday, in heaven, God will tell us why. God will explain it all to us, and we'll see it all clearly. We may not know now, but just be patient: someday all will be made known."

What exactly are such believers anticipating? That one day in heaven angels will escort us into a splendid lecture theater, the lights will go down, and a multimedia show of our former life will unfold, with God providing explanatory voice-over? Or perhaps that God instead will unroll the cosmic blueprints on the largest seminar table you've ever seen and walk us through them?

I have taken to offering a free cup of coffee to anyone who can provide me with a single verse of the Bible that supports this idea. Almost every time I have made such an offer someone will recall, if unclearly, the same New Testament verse, I Corinthians 13:12: "For now we see in a mirror, dimly, but then we will see face to face. Now I know only in part; then I will know fully, even as I have been fully known." "Aha!" he or she will say. "Bring on the espresso! Does this not prove that one day we will know all?"

Yet the chapter from which this verse is taken is the Apostle Paul's encomium on *love*. The focus of verse 12 is personal relationships ("face to face"), not abstract knowledge ("face to computer screen" or "face to flowchart"). The knowledge spoken of here clearly has to be personal knowledge of the beloved, not abstract knowledge of God's workings in earthly history.[3]

Is such a comprehensive explanation even possible? It seems likely, instead, that the phenomenon to be explained (namely, the global providence of God through history—or even in one's own life) is far too complicated to be grasped by the human intellect. Moreover, adequate comprehension and appropriate ethical evaluation of such complexity might well require a moral sensibility beyond human capacities. Philosopher Thomas Morris facetiously questions the credentials of critics who presume to understand and then pronounce upon the adequacy of God's administration of the entire cosmos. What he says about their limitations is true of all of us:

> [Questioners of God are often] people who don't have a clue as to what exactly they would do about the most pressing problems of their own city if they were mayor, or concerning the greatest difficulty facing their state if they were governor.

They would probably be quite hesitant if asked how precisely they would solve the greatest national crises if they were president, but they have no hesitation whatsoever in venturing to declare how they would solve what may be the single most troubling cosmic religious problem if they were God.[4]

The issue here, of course, is not God's ability to explain things to us. Presumably a Supreme Being has superb pedagogical skills. The problem instead lies in our relatively limited capacities to comprehend the matter at issue—God's supervision of the world—no matter how simply and extensively God might present it to us.[5] We might note that the very best minds devoted to this subject throughout history have failed to offer a theodicy with which even a majority of similarly interested experts could agree. Theodicy seems an extraordinarily difficult, and probably impossible, task.

Even if, however, we grant for the sake of argument that God could somehow convey all of this knowledge to us—and not just in heaven, either, but here and now—would a complete theodicy help us or hurt us in our progress toward "the point of it all"? Do we have strong grounds on which to suppose that providing such a complete theodicy would be a better way to achieve God's chief purpose of establishing relationships of trust and love and peace?

The Jewish, Christian, and Muslim Scriptures ought to give us respectful pause at this point. All three provide considerable information about God, and particularly about God in action on earth. Yet none of them provides a comprehensive theodicy. They do not declare any divine promise of such a theodicy. And in fact some stories show God manifestly refusing to offer explanations for divine actions even when specifically requested to do so by some of God's most exemplary followers.

The best-known such story is perhaps the ancient Jewish story of Job, to which an entire book is devoted in the Hebrew Scriptures (and Christian Old Testament). Poets and playwrights as well as theologians and rabbis have brooded over the depths of this text, but even its bare outlines can instruct us in our present discussion.

Job lived in the land of Uz in the Middle East many centuries before the time of Christ. (Whether Job was a historical character or not is a matter of long-standing dispute among scholars. As far as the Bible is concerned, though, he *could have been*, and we ought to read his story in this light.) Job lived a picture-perfect life of the righteous man who, because of the justice of God, enjoyed shalom in every respect: he was rich in livestock and servants; he was married and had ten grown children (seven sons, three daughters) who loved to be together and maintained a continual round of house parties for each other; and he cherished a consistent spiritual relationship with God.

An adversary, Satan, appears in the heavenly court and suggests that it is not the case that Job loves God and therefore enjoys blessing. Instead, Satan says, Job enjoys blessing and therefore loves God: "Does Job [reverence] God for nothing? Have you not put a fence around him and his house and all that he has, on every side? You have blessed the work of his hands, and his possessions have increased in the land" (Job 1:10 NRSV). Satan challenges God: reduce the blessing and you'll see a reduction in piety. Cut off the blessing, and Job will repudiate God entirely.

God takes Satan's bet, and poor Job is placed on the game board.[6] God allows Satan to "touch" all that Job has, although God forbids Satan from hurting Job's own person. Satan gets to work, and soon disasters rain down upon Job. A series of messengers brings bad news, each on the heels of the other with a worse message than the one before. The first messenger bursts in on Job and tells him that bandits have rustled his oxen and donkeys and killed the attending servants in the process. While the first messenger is still speaking, the second messenger interrupts to announce that "the fire of God" (perhaps a terrific electrical storm) has burst from the sky and destroyed the sheep and their tenders. The third messenger breaks in before the second has finished to announce that another tribal enemy has taken the camels and murdered the keepers. Finally, a fourth messenger appears with the most dreadful news of all: Job's loving sons and daughters, enjoying a meal at the eldest brother's home, now lie broken and dead under the rubble of the house blown down by a desert wind.

In four hammerblows, Job is destitute. He knows it, stands up, tears his clothes in the traditional Middle Eastern gesture of distress—and worships God. "Naked I came from my mother's womb, and naked shall I return there; the LORD gave, and the LORD has taken away; blessed be the name of the LORD" (1:20). Job recognizes a fundamental proposition: God is sovereign, and God is just. In these terrible events, God has simply taken back what God gave to Job freely in the first place. God owes Job nothing, so Job has no grounds to complain, and he does not.

Satan, however, remains unconvinced by Job's fortitude. He speaks to God again. "Skin for skin!" he cries. "All that people have they will give to save their lives. But stretch out your hand now and touch his bone and his flesh, and he will curse you to your face" (2:5). God again lets Satan go ahead, this time restricting him only from taking Job's life.

Satan immediately inflicts "loathsome sores" on Job, from scalp to toes. Job's wife cannot stand this latest curse, and urges Job to return a curse to God. "Do you still persist in your integrity?" she needles Job in exasperation. "Curse God and die" (2:9). But Job stands firm: "Shall we receive the good at the hand of God, and not receive the bad?" The narrative continues: "In all this, Job did not sin with his lips" (2:10).

Three acquaintances hear of Job's plight, and come to commiserate with him. For an entire week, they simply sit with him, sharing what they can of his horror in silence. Then Job breaks the silence and curses. But he does not curse God: he curses his own life. He now judges his misery to outweigh the goods he previously enjoyed, and thus condemns his life as ultimately negative.

His comrades respond, and for more than two dozen chapters, they go back and forth with Job, with one central disagreement becoming more and more intense. The friends stoutly maintain the goodness of God, and thus logically insist that Job must have sinned to have brought on his awful experiences. Job just as stoutly maintains his own goodness. He does *not* infer that God is unjust, but that God is at least *apparently* unjust and therefore does in fact owe Job something:

an explanation for God's actions and an exoneration of Job's behavior. (No one in the conversation raises the question of God's power. The narrative from start to finish simply assumes God's sovereignty to such an extent that even Satan's harm to Job is attributed in other verses to God's own action. God is the ultimate cause of all things, therefore God is the one who is ultimately behind Job's disasters.)

A fourth friend subsequently appears, and he chastises Job for his challenge to God. Job by this point has become furious with both God and his so-called comforters, and will not submit to this latest rebuke. He has known God for a long time, and this evil simply does not make sense. God has been his patron as Job has been God's servant. God ought to answer for these actions.

"Then the LORD answered Job," begins chapter 38. Job receives the divine audience he wanted, reminding us of the proverb to be careful what you wish for, since you just might get it. The LORD (that is, *Yahweh*, the personal name of God that is rendered "LORD" in most English translations) answers Job all right. But God answers Job on God's own terms and in God's own way. The LORD speaks—God meets Job where he is and communicates with him in words he can understand. But the LORD speaks "out of the whirlwind": God is invisible, alien, powerful, and certainly not Job's peer. And God makes sure from first to last that Job gets this point.

"Who is this that darkens counsel by words without knowledge?" God thunders (38:2). Stand up like a man, Job, and answer me. "Where were you when I laid the foundation of the earth? Tell me, if you have understanding" (38:4). Job wisely recognizes the question as rhetorical and keeps quiet. God proceeds to survey vast reaches of creation, from mountain goats to ocean monsters, from stars to wars, and declares sovereignty over all. So, God concludes, "Shall a faultfinder contend with the Almighty? Anyone who argues with God must respond" (40:2).

God's response to Job might seem manifestly unfair, a divine Debater blustering instead of answering, intimidating instead of informing, threatening instead of enlightening. But Job himself does not see it that way. "I know that you can do all things," Job replies. "I have uttered what I did not understand, things too wonderful for me, which I did not know. . . . I had heard of you by the hearing of the ear, but now my eye sees you; therefore I despise myself, and repent in dust and ashes" (42:2–6).

Job sees that God's answer is not an evasion, but in fact is a direct response to the ultimate question that neither Job nor his friends had considered: Do you know it all, and therefore stand in a position to judge God? It is one thing to grieve over one's own unhappiness; it is quite another thing to go on to pronounce judgment on God's administration of the world. Job cannot describe even how to make a horse or cause the rain to fall. Why does he thus presume competence to judge loftier matters of justice?

Job gets no insight from God as to why he suffered as he did. Indeed, the irony of the story is that we, as readers, are privy to the heavenly conversation between Satan and God that, mysterious as it is, gives us at least some clue as to why Job was cursed. The story gives no indication that righteous Job learns any of this. He certainly hears nothing of it when he asks God for answers.

What he does hear from God, however, is good enough for him. In the first place, he actually does hear from God. God does not forever remain aloof from a suffering servant. True, God does not answer on demand, but God does not leave Job alone forever in his distress. Second, God does address Job's questions, confusions, and fears. Whatever we might think of the adequacy of God's response, Job himself is satisfied with God's presence and the assertion of God's transcendent wisdom. Third, God vindicates Job in the eyes of his companions, and goes on to tell the first three that they have slandered not Job, ultimately, but God. They have spoken incorrectly about the way God works in the world: their strict equation of blessing and merit is far too simple and mechanical a view of how the sovereign Lord administers creation. God affirms instead that Job has spoken correctly, and God honors Job by telling these other three to ask Job to pray for them. Fourth, God restores Job's material fortunes twofold and grants him another ten children. (Some have seen in this latter blessing, perhaps wistfully, a hint of an afterlife in which Job would be reunited with his dead children as well, thus being blessed twofold in this respect also!)

We thus see that Job—and even his companions—weren't entirely wrong about the workings of the divine economy. God ultimately affirms Job's standing by giving him material and personal blessings. But Job and his friends were not entirely right. No human can say, "I have figured things out, and here's what God must and must not do." God alone knows all and decides justly in every situation, however odd and even contradictory at times the divine decisions may seem.

The Jewish Scriptures contain many similar stories in which a godly person calls out to God in protest. God is assumed to be both all-good and all-powerful, hence the believer's question: why are you acting, O Lord, in such an apparently contradictory way? Abraham asked, Moses asked, David asked, and many of the later prophets asked. In fact, one can see this questioning of God's goodness (again, no one ever questions God's power) as a major and recurring theme throughout these ancient books.

It is important to note several commonalities in these encounters. First, the believers call to God in their confusion and do so angrily. These are not polite requests for information, but cries from the heart for reassurance and, usually, rescue. (Indeed, the cry for reassurance is itself a cry for rescue: for rescue from doubt, from sinking into a cosmos that is out of the benevolent control of God.)

Second, God is rarely offended by this action. God does not blast any honest questioner with thunderbolts for impertinence. (God is not, however, pleased with Job's companions who only talk theology, who talk *about* God, rather than do what Job did along with his theologizing: pray *to* God.[7])

Third, God responds. In every single case, God responds to the sincere inquirer. God does not respond just when the questioner asks. God often makes the questioner wait, even to the verge of despair. Indeed, God might be testing the sincerity of the inquirer in such a delay. But God always responds—and *before* the inquirer finally gives up.

Fourth, God never fully explains the rationale for what God is doing—at best God gives but a partial explanation. This pattern of divine response without directly answering the question posed is striking. Why does God hold back? We can observe that when the Hebrew prophet Habakkuk *did* get a glimpse of the celestial blueprint, he did not like some of what he saw: God's ways continued to seem bewildering, even frightening. Even if we were capable of understanding more than we do of God's supervision of the world, knowing more wouldn't necessarily make a positive difference. A student of mine offered this pertinent wisdom: "Do we really want to know why? Would it help? If our child would have to die of cancer in order for us to gain heaven, who would want to know this?"[8] So we need to remember that God's reticence about explanations may be a mercy, not a curse.

Fifth, God nonetheless responds in a way that confirms and strengthens the faith of the desperate inquirer. God does this by acting, and by pointing to God's previous actions. There, for those ready to believe, is support for their faith. God does not expect Job to believe for no reason. Nor is Job's assent compelled by intimidation—although this is a common misunderstanding of God's appearance in the whirlwind. Instead, God lays out a catalog of divine actions at a level Job can appreciate, and Job draws the correct conclusion. God has set up the cosmos in a complex order well beyond Job's comprehension, and yet not beyond his appreciation. God knows a lot more than Job does, and yet what Job does see and understand of this catalog is beautiful, orderly, reassuring. So Job can trust God after all.[9]

Trust is the operative word. God does not overwhelm Job with an irrefutable case for divine goodness and wisdom. God overwhelms Job with majesty, yes, as an argument to warrant Job's deferential trust. But God does not unroll heavenly schematics and show Job that in fact God's way is the right way. Perhaps God does not do so because Job would, as we have discussed earlier, be as incapable as any other human being of grasping God's intricate design for the cosmos, or even God's design for Job's own life and those that touch it. So God instead makes this situation plain to Job and teaches him what Job *can* understand.

Some believers suggest that God would not give such a "showing" to Job for a different reason. If Job *were* indeed capable of comprehending God's undeniable wisdom, Job would have no logical choice: he would *have* to accept that God's way is right. But God does not act that way, such believers affirm. God does not want grudging acquiescence from people convinced against their will. God wants love from people who have been persuaded, yes, but who have chosen among *real options.* As Henri Blocher paraphrases John Hick, "faith will discover God's presence [and God's goodness and power] freely through ambiguous signs," not through compelling certainties.[10]

Whatever one thinks about this last matter, the general pattern of God's response to the question of evil, I suggest, points directly to the second option for God if God wants us to believe in divine goodness and power in the face of evil—and the second option for us in trying to decide how we can believe.

SUFFICIENT WARRANT

If God is not going to explain everything to us so that we can see for ourselves that Providence is doing right, and if God wants our faith to be *intelligent* and not blind, then God must provide us with some other intellectually satisfying grounds. We have already seen that God has given us at least partial answers to our questions. And those partial answers are not to be despised just because they don't resolve everything. Still, many of us need more. If God isn't going to show us what God is doing, then God needs to give us adequate reason to trust *anyway.* In short, God must provide us with grounds to trust *in spite of* evil, and in spite of our lack of a complete understanding of it.[11]

Consider an automobile mechanic. You consult him about a problem. He responds like this: "You have dirty spark plugs." You nod knowingly. "All you need is some new ones, and we have some on sale. You replace them yourself, or I can do it for you while you wait." The mechanic has explained the situation to your full satisfaction. You decide to reward his insight and his favoring you with a complete diagnosis by paying him to install the new plugs.

Suppose, however, the mechanic says something different. "You actually have a problem with your thrombulator that is affecting the discharging pressure of your whole ignition system. We can fix it, but it'll take a couple of days and some special parts." You know that *special*, in this lexicon, means *quite expensive*. But that's about all you know, since you've never heard of a "thrombulator"; nor does the concept of "discharging pressure" make any immediate sense to you.

Now you have to decide whether to trust the mechanic (unless, of course, you know enough about cars to recognize that I made up all of that automotive pseudo-terminology and it in fact means nothing). If you have just pulled off a major highway into a seedy-looking gas station thinking that you just needed your gas tank filled and your oil checked, and the attendant summons the mechanic without informing you first, and if I specify certain other conditions to fill out the story, you're likely going to distrust this stranger and drive to the next garage. On the other hand, if you have taken your car to the mechanic who, as far as you know, has given you reliable service for five years, and if the car *did* have some starting problems in the first place, then you may well simply hand over the keys. You are not irrational to do so, of course: you have *good reason* to believe him even as you do not *know* that he is telling the truth. Indeed, most of us probably would judge that you have *sufficient warrant* to trust him.

Each religion and each philosophy offers warrants to inquirers and believers. What each person must decide is whether those warrants are (a) sufficient for belief, especially in comparison with arguments *against* that religion or philosophy; and (b) whether the warrants for option X are stronger, and thus more worthy of assent than the warrants for options Y or Z. The rest of this chapter takes up the first of these two questions in regard to the Christian faith. Christianity will function as an example of a religion that provides warrants for belief in an all-good, all-powerful God in the face of evil. Judaism and Islam would mount their own versions of such an argument, of course: they, too, would argue that the evidence of God's love and God's trustworthiness are adequate for faith despite the evil around us that prompts us to doubt God.[12] But because my own main interest and expertise are in the Christian faith, and it is the religion to which I am personally committed, I shall confine my argument to that religion.

As for (b), each reader will have to decide for himself or herself as to the relative strengths of the case for Christianity vis-à-vis other intellectual and religious options. My purpose now simply is to see if Christianity can provide warrants sufficient for faith in God.

THE CASE FOR CHRISTIANITY IN JESUS CHRIST

As I have read through a good deal of historic and contemporary philosophy of religion on this subject and others, I have been struck by how rarely even Christian philosophers discuss Jesus Christ. Instead, the arguments usually seem confined to the severe choice between theism and atheism. There are often good reasons for such a restriction of field. But I have begun to wonder how the difficult problem of "God and evil" might be affected by bringing Jesus squarely into the picture.

Christians, after all, believe not only that Jesus was an important historical figure (as Jews do) or that Jesus was a prophet of God (as Jews do not, but Muslims do), but that Jesus was and is the actual human face of God: God in human form. Thus Christians through the centuries have elaborated a very simple, but immediately mysterious, concept they call the Trinity, or "tri-unity" of God: God is one God, but God exists in three "persons," Father, Son (who became human in Jesus Christ), and Holy Spirit. Each human being is just one person; God is three persons. Christians have devised many metaphors to show that something can be both three and one at the same time without contradiction, but the finest minds have agreed with the humblest: we have no exact parallel in our experience of a being that is simultaneously three in one, so we do not fully understand the Trinity.

Still, Christians affirm the Trinity as basic to their understanding of God, not least because they believe that they see God—not just messages from God, or the love of God, or even "godliness," but God—in the historical figure of Jesus of Nazareth. And so, to the scandal of Jews and Muslims, as well as to people of many other faiths, Christians do not merely respect or even revere Jesus, but they worship him as divine—without extending that status, as many Hindus happily would, for instance, to any other person or being. Christians are fierce monotheists: but their one God has three persons (a qualification that strikes Jews and Muslims, among others, as not "mysterious" but flatly contradictory!).

Now, this little excursion into Christian theology is vital to what follows. To cut directly to the bottom line: If we want to know what God is truly like, we can look at Jesus, for Jesus is God.

The great theologian Martin Luther was deeply troubled by the problem of evil.[13] In fact, Luther was more deeply troubled than most Christians or most non-Christians have been because he had a particular belief about God that many other theists do not. Luther believed in predestination, which (simply put) means that God sovereignly, and without explanation to us, decides which humans God will save from sin (and thus welcome into heaven) and which humans God shall leave in sin (and thus condemn to hell). Luther, like his follower John Calvin, found this idea repellent: Calvin called it the decretum horribile, the terrible decree of God. Luther and Calvin agree, in fact, with their critics who find this idea an awful thing to predicate of God. Still, they believed it because they believed that the Bible taught it.

Believing in predestination as they did, Martin Luther and John Calvin found the question of God and evil more challenging than many others ever do. For in other Christian theologies, God can "make up" in the next life for whatever evils one suffers in this life. Indeed, God has all eternity to make up for any miseries in one's temporary earthly career. But if God has foreordained some persons never to be rescued, then they have no prospect of anything being "made up" to them. They are doomed forever. To both Luther and Calvin, the idea that the God they loved would act in such an apparently arbitrary way was utterly appalling. But they felt compelled to maintain this belief from their reading of Scripture, so they had to find some way to preserve faith in the goodness and power of God.

Whether or not one agrees with the doctrine of predestination is not important here. What is relevant is that two such theological giants were forced to consider the question of God and evil in a particularly stark and extreme form, and their response to this challenge is helpful to all who are interested in Christian thought.

The God of predestination, the God of worldwide providence, the God who created all and sustains all and thus ultimately is responsible for all—this God has revealed to us only glimpses of the divine cosmic plan. God has not let us see in any comprehensive way the sense in suffering, the method in the madness. God has chosen, instead, to remain hidden in mystery. Those inquirers who attempt to climb ladders of empirical observation and rationalist deduction in order to peer into the mind of this hidden God will find only a vertiginous abyss, an apparent chaos they can never plumb. Indeed, Luther believed, such foolhardy speculators risk both their sanity (for the ways of God will confuse them) and their faith (for the ways of God might dismay them).

Thus, Luther counseled, one must "flee the hidden God and run to Christ." Now this advice sounds, strictly speaking, like heresy, for Christians are supposed to believe that the hidden God and the God-who-is-in-Jesus are the same God. So how can one "flee" from one and "run" to another as if they were two separate divinities between whom one could choose?

Luther's point precisely depends, however, upon orthodox Trinitarianism. It is just because the two Gods are one and the same God that his advice works. One must run away from the mysteries of God's providence about which we cannot know enough to understand (because God has revealed so little about them), and run toward Jesus Christ in whom we find God adequately revealed.

Now, "adequately" sounds rather unimpressive. Why not "fully" or "comprehensively" revealed? I say "adequately" exactly because God has not fully revealed God's entire mind and ways to us in Jesus. Notably, God has not revealed through Jesus why some people suffer and some people do not. But God has revealed Godself in Jesus in a manner completely adequate for faith. And that, we recall, is "the point of it all." That is what human life is about, and what God has provided for in Jesus. In

Jesus we see what we desperately need to see: God close to us, God active among us, God loving us, God forgiving our sin, God opening up a way to a new life of everlasting love. If Jesus is the human face of God, Christians affirm, then human beings have a God who cares, a God who acts on their behalf (even to the point of self-sacrifice), and a God who is now engaged in the complete conquest of evil and the reestablishment of universal shalom for all time. If Jesus is truly God revealed, then we can trust God in spite of the evil all around us and in us.

The religious and existential questions come together in this entirely satisfactory answer. In the face of evil, God in Jesus declares Godself to us, touches us through the love of others, speaks to us through the Bible and in prayer, and provides for our needs with our ultimate benefit always in view. We can trust God both when we understand at least something of why some evils occur, and also when we don't have a clue. Yes, God can seem remote and impassive when we read about a tragedy in the newspaper or experience suffering ourselves—but can we imagine Jesus Christ not near and not caring, not doing all he can and should to help, however mysterious that help might be to us? We can respond properly to evil in our lives because *we know that God is all-good and all-powerful because we know Jesus.*

The religious and existential satisfaction of knowing God in Jesus, however, depends upon a satisfactory answer to the intellectual question. One might well have read this far and been prepared, at least for argument's sake, to grant the proposition that if Jesus is God's ultimate Word to humankind, if Jesus is God made human, *then* God is thus revealed as a wholly beneficent and omnipotent God. But the first contention needs warrant. Is it *true* that Jesus is God in human form? What intellectually persuasive warrants can be offered for this assertion?

THE CHRISTIAN STORY

Before examining the warrants for Christianity, however, we must first get clear on what Christianity is. Many North Americans and Europeans are quite confident that they understand Christianity, whether or not they go to church. But poll data show that most people in these parts of the world are ignorant of even the basic contours of the faith.[14] So let us make sure that we are talking about the same thing when we are assessing the merits of Christianity.

One way to get at the essence of the Christian religion is to consider the Christian account of the world, the cosmic narrative in which the entire history of the world and all who live in it is placed. By tracing out this story, we will gather up resources that will help us understand a Christian response to evil.

The Christian religion tells this story in four parts. The first part is briefly rendered but glorious. It is the Creation of the world. Christians accept the Jewish Scriptures as their own, since they see Christianity as the fulfillment of Biblical Judaism, and so take as divinely given revelation the story of Creation in the first book of the Bible, Genesis. Christians thus believe with Jews that "In the beginning, God created the heavens and the earth" (Genesis 1:1). Christians interpret this story their own way, naturally, and some passages in the New Testament look back upon and provide additional insight into the Creation story. But Christians agree with Jews on some fundamental principles in this account.

The first is that God alone created everything else. There are no other gods, no other creative principles, no other self-existent beings in the universe. Whatever existed and whatever now exists does so because of the will and power of God alone.

Second, God created the cosmos and pronounced it "good" at each stage. God did not create anything evil, nor anything that was somehow *both* good and evil. All that God created was good, from the sun to the oceans to plants and animals.

Third, God created human beings as unique in this world. They (male and female together—the Bible is clear on this point) would bear the very image of God. Indeed, they would "image" God to the rest of creation. In their work as gardeners of God's good earth, caretakers and shapers of the world, they would, so to speak, continue God's creative work through their own. An unbiased reading of Genesis 1 and 2, by the way, gives no support to the widespread misunderstanding that Christianity somehow licenses the exploitation of the earth by humanity. The Genesis account of creation is actually profoundly, if tersely, ecological. There is one earth, one integrated society, and human beings are to take their places in it as resident caretakers—not as marauders.

In the Genesis account, God says something special about human beings that God does not say about any other creature: they are "very good." But they do not stay "very good" for long. The second part of the Christian story, sadly, is told in the third chapter of Genesis, after just two brief chapters to sketch the nascent shalom of Creation. And this second part is the tragedy of what is traditionally termed the *Fall*.

This ancient story has been widely told and frequently misunderstood. Though its profundities have yet to be fully fathomed, its basic contours are fairly clear. God gives Adam and Eve full proprietorial control over the garden, offering them any plant they like for food. One tree, however, God places off limits: the tree of the knowledge of good and evil. (The Bible does not explain whether this tree possessed some extraordinary quality that bestowed such knowledge, or whether such knowledge would come simply from making the moral decision to disobey God and eat its otherwise ordinary fruit.)

Now a serpent comes onto the scene for the first time and begins to converse with Eve. Nothing in the story indicates that Eve is startled by this. Perhaps the serpent was one of several animals with whom Adam and Eve spoke, or perhaps the serpent was peculiarly gifted with speech. Eve does not remark on the serpent's speaking, but on its speech. When challenged by the serpent, she misstates God's proscription, making it both slightly more demanding than it was (Eve says that God told them not even to touch the tree, which God did not say; only eating the fruit was expressly forbidden) and slightly less definite (Eve says that God told them not to disobey "in case" or "lest" they die; God said that they would *surely* die). The serpent, as if seeing in these small distortions of God's clear instructions a wavering in Eve's resolution to obey God, flatly denies God's word to the humans. "You will not die," the serpent assures Eve. "God is preventing you, in fact, from becoming gods yourselves, knowing good and evil."

There is no indication in the story that Eve considered just why God would lie to them or seek to prevent them from enjoying the knowledge of good and evil. There is no indication that she considered the relative reliability and authority of the serpent versus the reliability and authority of God. There is no indication that Eve considered that perhaps she knew what good was *already*, so that an increase in her knowledge of "good and evil" could only be negative: she would know what disobedience was. Furthermore, she would *really* know what evil was through personal experience—personal experience being a common emphasis in the ancient Hebrew concept of knowledge. Eve may well have considered any or all of these things. But in the compressed language of this ancient story, what Eve *does* consider is the pleasing appearance of the fruit: it surely *looked* both beautiful and tasty. And that seemed enough. She ate it.

Adam, offered the fruit by his wife, appears at least as unreflective as she does. He takes what she gives him and eats it. And things change. Everything changes. Adam and Eve look at each other and at themselves in a new way. They now know both good and evil, and they don't like this new knowledge. They are ashamed of their nakedness, of their utter openness to each other, to the world, and to God. And in an extraordinarily powerful gesture, Adam and Eve sit down together and work to cover themselves by stitching pitiful aprons of leaves. Minute by minute they work, fumblingly and blushingly and painstakingly putting together something, *anything*, to hide within.

God arrives for what seems to be a regular afternoon visit (the story does not say what form God takes). Adam is not at the appointed spot, and God calls for him—as if God doesn't know! Adam replies that he is hiding because he is naked and ashamed (perhaps because it was sadly obvious that mere aprons would not suffice to conceal all that Adam wanted hidden from God's gaze). God then confronts the main issue: "Who told you you were naked?" Who told you, that is to say, that you were in some particular condition and that you ought to be in another one instead? "Did you eat of the tree from which I forbade you to eat?"

Adam tells the truth. But he does it in a way that blames both his wife (so much for marital solidarity, alas, even in sin) and, implicitly, God as well, since God had created the wife expressly as a companion for Adam. "The woman that you gave to be with me gave me the fruit," Adam says, "and I ate."

God wastes no time confronting this disappointing answer, and turns to the woman. "Well, what is this that you have done?"

The woman, now seeing her husband in a new light, follows his lead and replies in kind, "The serpent tricked me, and I ate."

God then turns to the serpent, and proceeds directly to judgment. (Perhaps God was well familiar with the serpent and needed to ask it no questions.) God curses the serpent and, in particular, destroys the little relationship the serpent had begun with the woman, to her lasting cost. God promises to put enmity between the serpent and the woman and between the serpent's descendants and the woman's descendants. (Many later interpreters have seen all of this as having to do with spiritual warfare between Satan and humanity, but the text itself is enigmatic.)

Then God shows the woman and the man something of the consequences of their actions. Their archetypal functions as parents and gardeners, as they were to obey God's Creation injunction to "be fruitful and multiply and tend the earth," will carry on, but now with difficulty. The good work God had called them to do will continue, but now in a nature that resists them. Childbirth will be made terribly painful, and gardening will become grinding labor: "cursed is the ground because of you; in toil you shall eat of it all the days of your life; thorns and thistles it shall bring forth for you; and you shall eat the plants of the field. By the sweat of your face you shall eat bread until you return to the ground" (Genesis 3:17–19). Shalom between humanity and nature is broken. Furthermore, shalom between husband and wife is damaged, as male domination emerges for the first time in their marriage.

Finally, God sends them out of the garden entirely. For, God says, the serpent was correct in a perverse way. The humans *did* become like gods, knowing good and evil, but they know it from the vantage of the wrong side of the divide between good and evil. And because they are in this terrible state of sin, God concludes, they must be prevented from eating of the tree of life (*another* mysterious tree) and thereby living forever in that wretched condition. Mercifully, then, God sends them away.

Life, of a sort, continues outside the garden. The very next verse shows Adam and Eve conceiving their first son and the following verses show another son joining his brother as caretakers of nature (Cain as a gardener, Abel as a shepherd). But the mark of sin is upon them all, and the subsequent chapters of Genesis follow a spreading stain of evil as the human race proliferates: from Cain's envious fratricide to God's final destruction of the entire polluted human population, save Noah and his family, in the great Flood. The harmonious goodness of the original creation disintegrates, deteriorates, destroys, and dies. This sorry part of the Christian story, then, is the primeval Fall from shalom.

Let's pause for some candid reflection. Doesn't this all sound unbelievable, like a fairy story for kids rather than a serious explanation of reality for adults? Faithful Christians disagree about just how literally to take the Genesis tales. Philosopher Peter Kreeft, however, directs our attention to the central issue: "The myth says that we suffer and [yet] find this outrageous, we die and find this natural fact unnatural, because we dimly remember Eden." This story of Creation and Fall strangely resonates with our deepest longings for things as they should be, with our deepest sense that things as they are, are not right. Could the story possibly, on some basic level, be true?[15]

Christianity clings to the promise that judgment is not God's final word upon humanity. Christianity looks back on its Jewish/Israelite heritage, and sees God select a man and a woman, Abraham and Sarah, from whom a chosen nation descends. This nation's history will serve as an object lesson to all nations: God is good and wants to bless; those who respond with gratitude and cooperation reap blessing after blessing; those who respond with disdain and rejection reap curse after curse. The histories of other nations may or may not teach moral precepts, but the history of the nation of Israel rolls out as a banner of fundamental truth. God keeps promises; God rewards the righteous; God punishes the evil.

Still, this strict justice is not God's final word either. For God preserves Israel even in the face of Israel's frequent betrayals. God remains faithful to Israel despite Israel's spiritual adultery (in the dramatic metaphor used by the prophets). More than this, God promises through the prophets, time after time, over several hundred years, to lift Israel to a position of spiritual, moral, economic, and political health such as Israel has never known. And God promises to do this through a specially appointed person, one who will combine the offices of prophet, priest, and king (some of whose incumbents were recognized in ancient Israel by the rite of anointing with oil, and thus were *messiahs*) into the office of Messiah—the Anointed.

Devout Jews today continue to wait for Messiah to come. Many Jews believe that it is the nation of Israel collectively that is personified in the figure of Messiah. Other Jews look for a particular individual. Christians believe they have found him already—or, better, that *he* found *them*. That is why Christians call Jesus of Nazareth *Christ*, from the Greek word for *Messiah*. Why do Jews and Christians have such a fundamental disagreement over the same person? Because they have quite good reasons to disagree over this singular individual.

Jesus did not have the career that Jews of first-century Palestine expected Messiah to have. Yes, he worked wonders, miracles that showed supernatural power at work in his life. Yes, he aligned himself with the Scriptures and taught as a respected, if uncredentialed, rabbi. Yes, he seemed to have considerable personal charisma, speaking with an extraordinary individual authority. But Jesus failed to accomplish the most basic task of Messiah. Indeed, he seemed positively uninterested in it. He did not free his people from their bondage to imperial Rome. He did not set up an independent kingdom to recall the glories of David and Solomon. He had virtually nothing to do with politics until his own trial and execution. And he was executed by the state: some Messiah! In short, for all of his admirable qualities (and many Jews will allow that Jesus had some), *he was a failure as Messiah*. He did not look like whom they were expecting—even given the considerable differences among Jewish Messianic expectations. Jesus did not look like *anybody's* idea of Messiah.[16]

To this day, Jesus does not look like what many people want in a

Savior. He does not offer to free them immediately from all oppression and obligation. He does not offer to make them financially secure. He does not offer to provide them with unending comfort and pleasure. He does not offer to settle their scores, to promote their interests, to do their bidding.

Yet Christians—millions of them, all over the globe, across lines of culture, class, race, and sex—have found in Jesus of Nazareth exactly what and whom they *need*, even if not what (they thought) they wanted. For Christians believe that God, through Jesus, is bringing about the eventual deliverance of the whole world. Christians believe that God's plan of salvation reached its decisive moment in the career of Jesus of Nazareth, and that it is now working out slowly, but surely, to the ends of the earth. Christians believe that in Jesus of Nazareth, God established once and for all the basis for the renewal of God's spoiled, sick creation and is now at work to accomplish it fully.

So what *did* God do in Jesus, at the focus of this third part of the Christian story, the stage of Redemption? In particular, what did God do about sin and evil?

Christianity stresses five stages of the life of Jesus, which we can call Incarnation, Inauguration, Crucifixion, Resurrection, and Ascension. First, God became human, literally becoming "flesh" (*carne*, in Latin). Christians do not pretend to understand all of what is meant by this stupendous claim. Over centuries they have tried to clarify what they mean partly by ruling out what they do *not* mean. Jesus was not, first, a ghost or other apparition. He was not a kind of heavenly hologram. He was fully human physiologically: he ate, slept, walked, talked, and—ultimately—died. If God was to reach down and save us, God would have to become one of us. So Christians affirm that God became truly human. Jesus' mother, Mary, became pregnant through God's miraculous power, but Jesus was born in the normal way, raised in the normal way, and lived in the normal way. He was a human being.

Second, Jesus was more than a human being. Many people who are not themselves Christian have gladly recognized in Jesus an outstanding individual. They have respected his courage, followed some of his teachings, and acclaimed him as a great man. But authentic Christians insist on going further than this. They insist that the only way to make sense of the whole career of Jesus of Nazareth—his life, death, later appearances, and final, abrupt disappearance—is to go well beyond respecting or even revering Jesus, to actually *worship* him. Now, the first Christians were staunch Jews and thus staunch monotheists who worshiped only one God. Thus they concluded that if Jesus was to be worshiped, as they believed he had to be, then Jesus had to be more than a prophet, or wonder worker, or even an angel. Jesus of Nazareth *had to be God*.[17] In this way, Christians came to understand that God had two aspects or personalities or ego centers or *somethings* (Christians have never been able to agree on the exact nature of God's plurality in unity): God was at least two in one. (Later Christians came to understand that God is actually three in one, a Trinity, as they determined that the Holy Spirit of God constituted the third member of what theologians call the Godhead.)

The bottom line, in any case, is firm and clear. In Jesus of Nazareth, we have God. We have not only a messenger from God, a representative of God, an example of devotion to God, a teacher of God's truth, a conveyor of God's power—*we have God*. How this can be—how God's being and human being, how God's psyche and a human psyche, can be one individual—is something no reasonable Christian claims to understand. To be fair, however, let us remember that the best scientific minds today are a long way from fully explaining even *human* psychology yet. And still we all continue to believe that human beings in fact have psyches, and we continue to have important dealings with the human psyche in all sorts of ways. We believe that human beings have psyches not because we can fully describe and explain them, but because we have such strong evidence of their presence and activity. It is by similar logic that the early Christians concluded that in Jesus Christ they confronted the very presence and activity of God.

We do not know whether the baby Jesus gave evidence of his extraordinary nature even to his devoted parents Mary and Joseph. Christmas crèche scenes to the contrary, the Bible does not report that the infant Jesus glowed in his manger, or that he and his parents were adorned with haloes. He likely looked and acted like every other newborn. Furthermore, despite some fanciful stories about the young Jesus in certain ancient Christian literature, the authoritative Gospels give us only glimpses of his birth and growing-up years. We do not encounter Jesus otherwise until his public ministry begins, around the age of thirty. This public service begins the second stage of Jesus' life, the *inauguration* of the Kingdom of God.

Christians believe that God is always ultimately in control of the world, as God is the basis of all existence everywhere. But in the career of Jesus of Nazareth—in his words, his miracles, his encounters with all sorts of people, his model of service to others, his majestic superiority cloaked in kind humility—is the beachhead, the foothold, the first ground staked out in God's great project to reclaim the cosmos from the evil that corrupts it. (Indeed, and especially in Eastern Orthodox versions of Christianity, the Incarnation itself—the event of God becoming human in Jesus—is understood to bridge the gap between the divine and the mortal; thus Jesus from his very conception begins the project of drawing human beings upward into the life of God.) In the public career of Jesus, as he touched people with gentleness and healing, as he spoke with unparalleled authority and aptness, as he moved with steadfast purpose toward his final confrontation with the powers of his day, we see flashes of God's pure shalom amid the swirling murk of our world.

This is what Jesus meant when he proclaimed that "the kingdom of God is at hand." Jesus' life inaugurated God's direct and uncompromised rule on earth, a rule (or "kingdom") that would extend outward from its original ground in Jesus to claim the allegiance of Jesus' faithful disciples (such as Peter and Mary Magdalene) and, through their own lives and testimony, the allegiance of individuals and nations across the globe. Evil human beings, with the assistance of evil spiritual powers, would resist the advance of this kingdom. Sometimes they would halt it, perhaps through one or the other of their favorite strategies, persecution and subversion. Sometimes they would even seem to turn it back for a time. But Jesus' life marks the irreversible beginning of the end for evil and the beginning of the eternal reign of God on the earth God once made and has always cared for. And, as the Jewish Bible prophesied of Messiah, "his kingdom shall have no end"—not in time, or in space.

Jesus' life, though, did have an end. And it was an end that scandalized Jews and, later, Muslims. Messiahs and prophets of the true God might be misunderstood and unappreciated by God's people and even by the religious leaders themselves. There was, after all, a long history of God's spokespersons being rejected by Israel before Jesus came on the scene, and Muḥammad himself found it impossible to win a hearing from his native city of Mecca until he came in force with the Medinan army. But an authentic Jewish Messiah or a true Muslim prophet *does not ultimately fail*. Whatever setbacks he might encounter along the way, God's blessing upon his work guarantees that he will finally succeed in every respect. For how can God's own representative, backed by God's own power as he executes God's own will, possibly fail? Thus Jews reject Jesus as Messiah, and Muslims reject the Christian account of Jesus' last days—he did not suffer and die as the Christians say; he escaped all of it by the mercy of Allāh.

Christians entirely agree with the basic presupposition of their Jewish and Muslim friends: God's anointed ones *do* succeed in their callings. But Christians view this last stage of Jesus' life differently—*very* differently. For Christians, Jesus' abject humiliation before Jewish and Roman courts, Jesus' rejection by his own people and by the imperial government of the day, Jesus' vulnerability to the taunts of common soldiers and execution watchers, and Jesus' long and agonizing death by crucifixion all are signs that point to his ultimate glory as God's own Son, not symbols of his rejection by God.

For in this third stage of Jesus' life, symbolized in the Crucifixion, Christians see the decisive event in God's work of reclaiming and restoring the world. The cross of Jesus does not disqualify him as Messiah. This event above all entitles Jesus to be called *Christos*, God's true servant. In three of the four Gospels, Jesus explicitly ties together his messiahship with his death and resurrection (Matthew 16:16–21; Mark 8:29–31; Luke 9:20–22). The cross is part of Christ's saving work on our behalf. It is at once both his greatest humiliation and greatest glory.

In the Crucifixion, Christians through the ages have seen several wonderful things. They have seen an example of dedication to a cause, a martyr willing even to suffer and die for his principles. Second, they have seen a display of God's love. In the brutal pinioning of wrists to wood, "God's arms are flung wide to embrace the world." Third, they have seen the Deity identifying personally with the victims of oppression. Many people subscribe to the idea that God is somehow remote and unfeeling, and just bosses us around in our miserable world from a comfortable throne in heaven. No! says the cross of Christ. *God knows what it is to suffer.*

This last point deserves elaboration. God suffers along with us, yes, and all suffering grieves God's heart. But God also suffered directly in the life and death of Jesus. God experienced what we experience firsthand, in the flesh. We must never forget that when we argue with God about our own suffering or that of others. *God has been there.* Dorothy Sayers put this point well:

> For whatever reason God chose to make man as he is—limited and suffering and subject to sorrows and death—he [God] had the honesty and the courage to take his own medicine. Whatever game he is playing with his creation, he has kept his own rules and played fair. He can exact nothing from man that he has not exacted from himself. He has himself gone through the whole of human experience, from the trivial irritations of family life and the cramping restrictions of hard work and lack of money to the worst horrors of pain and humiliation, defeat, despair, and death. When he was a man, he played the man. He was born in poverty and died in disgrace and thought it well worthwhile.[18]

Above all, however, Christians have affirmed that *on the cross, things changed.* Mysterious as it remains even to the wisest minds, the fundamental Christian affirmation is that the cross of Jesus doesn't just *show* us things, it *did* something once and for all. That is why it was necessary: not merely as a symbol pointing to something else (the love and sympathy of God, the enormity of human sin), but as a world-changing event that did indeed direct the love and sympathy of God to deal effectively with the enormity of human sin.

Two principal images have been used by Christians to explain what Jesus accomplished on the cross: Christ as Sacrifice, and Christ as Victor.[19] The former harks back to the extensive symbolism of Israelite temple worship, in which animals were killed and offered to God as substitutes for the human sinners who gave them up. "Life for life" was the basic principle, because sin at its root is the enemy of life. The Hebrew prophets themselves made clear that these rituals together formed an elaborate picture of God's holiness (God views sin as mortally serious, and therefore the most graphic symbolism of life and death was necessary to portray its cost and its redemption) and God's mercy (God was willing to accept animal substitutes, although it makes no logical or moral sense to do so: how can the blood of bulls or goats possibly make up for human sin?). The ultimate payment for, the ultimate cost of, human sin had to be borne *by human beings*.

For God could hardly say, "Okay, you seem sorry, so let's just forget about it." Convenient as that might seem to us, such a scenario fails to take sin seriously. *And we ourselves agree* that another sort of response is appropriate if it is *somebody's else's* forgiveness at issue. Adolf Hitler and Josef Stalin are the favorite examples in our century, but think of the evil person of your choice. Does it not offend your sense of justice to imagine such an individual standing before the judgment of God, merely professing remorse for sins committed, and then God directly ushering him or her into eternal bliss?

We know we are to be forgiving, but many of us tend to feel instead that at least particularly wicked individuals ought to get their just deserts. "They oughta pay," some of us tend to think, even if it's not entirely clear to us (a) just what they ought to "pay"; (b) to whom they owe such payment; or (c) what good their suffering, after afflicting others with suffering, does—do two sets of suffering make a right? As Dostoyevsky's Ivan Karamazov exclaims, "What use is vengeance to me, what use to me is hell for torturers, what can hell put right again, when those children have been tortured to death?"[20] These are deep waters indeed.

Perhaps, however, some other way of considering this whole question makes more sense than the language (admittedly enshrined in Christian tradition) of debt and payment, or perhaps takes up this language into a higher metaphor. For clearly the question of what sin is and how it should be atoned for is not a question of money, nor is it even (as medieval theologian Anselm of Canterbury famously put it) a question of restoring God's honor after the affront it has suffered from human disobedience. The problem of sin most basically is that it is an offense against God, and especially against God's desire to enjoy a loving relationship with us. Sin repudiates that desire and that relationship. Sin rejects God, hurts God's feelings, scorns God's attempts at reconciliation. To put it in contemporary language that is no more coarse than that used in the Jewish prophetic Scriptures themselves, sin dumps God and sleeps with the enemy.

What God has done through the ages of such abuse, and what God does supremely in Jesus on the cross, is what all of us do when we forgive. God absorbs the pain. God bears the shame. God swallows the anger, and opens up the divine arms to us again. Anyone who asks, "Why doesn't God just forgive? Why does anyone have to suffer— Jesus or anyone else?" has never forgiven a serious offense. Forgiveness *costs* the forgiver.

Let's return for a moment to the more elementary language of financial transactions (and we can thus see why this language is traditionally popular in such discussion, and also why it is so limited). I owe you a thousand dollars. I cannot pay you. You can take me to court and try to make me pay you, but I truly have no resources to do so. So (in some legal systems) you can press charges and have me punished in prison for failing to pay my debt. But you aren't any richer for doing so, are you? My going to prison might quench your thirst for vengeance, but it doesn't deal with the debt.

Your other choice is to forgive the loan. What this means, strictly speaking, is that *you pay yourself the thousand dollars on my behalf*. Now no responsible bookkeeping in the world is going to make such a transaction "zero out." You will always have a net loss of a thousand dollars. What you have done, though, is remove my name from the list of debtors and taken the loss yourself.

We can now see one important reason why the doctrine of the Trinity—apparently such an odd, even contradictory, idea—is vital to the Christian understanding of things. If God and Jesus are different beings, then Jesus on the cross looks like just one more scapegoat being punished for the sake of other humans' sins. Indeed, now we would have Christianity championing human sacrifice. And we would have the same conundrum we had before: how can punishing someone else possibly suffice for my offenses? Some feminist theologians have accused this Christian doctrine of "substitutionary atonement" (as this basic idea is formally termed) of sanctioning child abuse: God the Father victimizes his Son. If the doctrine of the Trinity is stoutly affirmed, however, then it is God who hangs on the Cross. It is the one God who bears the rejection of the world. It is the one God who forgives humanity our sin of ingratitude, who "takes it" without reprisal, who drinks to the last drop our poisonous betrayal.[21]

It is an utter mystery even to the best Christian minds how all of the sin of all of humanity could be funneled into that single episode of Jesus' suffering and death. Perhaps, though, we can see at least that God has endured the very worst we could deal out. God has faced the most degrading humiliation, the most heartrending rejection, the most complete dishonor possible, and received it with unquenched love for us all. This is the true sacrifice of forgiveness.

The image of Christ as Victor speaks of Jesus conquering the enemies of the human race and of the whole created order, and thus the enemies of God: sin, evil, and death. It looks instead, of course, as if Jesus is the utterly vanquished victim, not the supremely successful victor. Perhaps, though, we can understand something of the mystery of Christ's triumph like this:

A warrior is expected to defeat his opponent by inflicting a wound so severe that it renders response impossible. This aggressive power is what the Jews expected in their Messiah. In comparison a crucified Jesus looks like just the opposite. A warrior, however, could theoretically defeat his opponent in at least one other way. Instead of hammering his opponent into submission, a warrior could choose instead to stand still and take his enemy's best blow—indeed, to absorb all of his blows, one after the other, until the enemy literally exhausts his power and collapses, spent. If the warrior is still standing, he is the victor without taking a single aggressive action.

This is what Jesus did on the cross. He suffered the worst that evil could hurl at him: rejection by his own beloved people in the streets of their capital city; hatred from the experts in his own religion; injustice at the hands of the Roman court; disloyalty and betrayal from two of his closest associates, Judas and Peter, and abandonment by almost all the rest of his followers; the public shame of being stripped naked and ridiculed as a preposterous "King of the Jews"; agony in the exquisite torture of crucifixion; and the constant pressure of temptation to give it all up, to smash these ungrateful creatures with the thunderbolts of heaven, to start again with a new race, to stand up for himself and act like a god. Instead, Jesus acted like *God* and stayed there, taking on himself the sins of the world like a boulder on his back, holding himself in place (for none other could hold him) as his opponents inflicted their worst. Finally, he died, and the suffering ended. The ultimate question then was posed. Who would get up off the floor of the arena? Which champion would prevail?

The disciples of Jesus were convinced that death had prevailed. And death, as everyone knows, never loses its grip. Yes, they had seen Jesus raise other people from the dead. But Jesus himself was dead: who would raise him? All four gospel accounts make clear that Jesus' followers were convinced that he was finished, his broken body awaiting proper burial in a friend's tomb.

Yet when several of his followers arrived at his grave at first light on the Sunday morning following his crucifixion, they found him gone. One, a special friend named Mary, actually encountered Jesus in the garden of the tomb, and in a moment became convinced that he had not only come back from the dead, but had somehow become even more vital, more powerful, more alive than ever. Jesus told her to tell his other disciples that he had conquered death, the final enemy of humankind, and offered resurrection to everyone who would trust him for it.

The concept of resurrection is the key to Christian hope. It does not mean reincarnation. Those who believe in reincarnation understand there to be a spiritual self or soul that progresses through a cycle of birth, death, and rebirth, taking on a new body each time. Nor does resurrection mean "resuscitation," as if Jesus had experienced something like cardiac arrest for a short time and was then "brought back" through some unknown means. The concept of resurrection means that Jesus' whole self, physical and psychospiritual, was transformed into a new mode of existence. The old body was transformed into the new body, therefore witnesses reported that Jesus' tomb was empty. Indeed, the graveclothes were still lying there as if Jesus' body had metamorphosed and disappeared right through them.

What happened to Jesus, Christians believe, also will happen to all who love and trust him. Some day after their death, when Christ returns in the final stage of the cosmic drama, the blessed dead will rise with renewed bodies matched with renewed souls, fit for the enjoyment of the new life God has prepared for them. Because Jesus conquered death in the power of God, he stands now as victor over death and all lesser enemies of humankind. Indeed, because death was the most evil even Satan could have wished upon the Son of God, Satan, too, was defeated in the resurrection of Jesus, as Satan will be ultimately vanquished in the resurrection of all of God's people.[22]

Following his resurrection, Jesus appeared among his now-delighted (if also astonished and fearful) disciples for short periods of teaching and encouragement. After a few weeks, however, he met them on the Mount of Olives, just outside the ancient city of Jerusalem, to bid them good-bye. He commissioned them to go out as his messengers ("apostles" means "ones who are sent"), bringing the good news of God's saving power offered to everyone who would believe. He promised to return someday, to wrap up this stage of human history in the final judgment of evil and the rescue of his people.

In the meanwhile, he said, the project of Redemption would continue through spiritual and human extensions of himself. The Holy Spirit, Jesus promised, would soon come upon the disciples and unite them into the Church, the metaphorical Body of Christ, God's main agent of proclamation and healing in the world. As God had reached the world through the spirit and body of Jesus of Nazareth, now God would continue to draw the world out of evil and toward fellowship with God through the Holy Spirit empowering Christ's Body on earth, the Christian Church. Following this stupendous promise (particularly stupendous given the small, motley collection of disciples to whom it was given on a Judean hilltop), Jesus symbolized his return to heavenly authority and power by literally rising straight up into the air, as if he was going "up" to heaven, until a cloud finally obscured him from sight. This *ascension*, then, was the final visible act of God in Jesus, an act that drove home to the disciples the status of their Lord and the solemn importance of their assignment.

The third stage of the Christian story, the stage of Redemption, thus entered a new phase in which God would extend the salvation secured at the center by the work of Jesus out into all the world through the work of the Church. For almost two thousand years, Christians therefore have worshiped Jesus and invited others to do so, and served needy human beings in his name—that is, as representatives of Jesus. Many, many times, sadly, Christians have performed their job as ambassadors poorly. Those calling themselves Christians at times have repudiated the spirit of their Master by committing atrocities—whether Crusaders in battle, or abusive parents at home—and claiming their deeds as Christian all the while. Christians also have committed sins of omission, failing to do good when opportunities arose. Philip Yancey, himself a Christian, chides the Church in this vein: "God's reliance on the church almost guarantees that disappointment with God will be permanent and epidemic."[23]

Still, other Christians have patiently, often unobtrusively and on a small scale, brought good news in word and deed to victims of the world's evil. And in such love the good news of God's own love reaches further and further around the globe. In such actions, the work of Jesus truly extends outward from his life, death, resurrection, and ascension to embrace the world. And the goodness and power of God seem more credible, more real, than before.

The final stage of the Christian story was promised by Jesus himself. Before Jesus' day it was foreseen by Israelite prophets, and after his departure it was foreseen again by Christian ones. When Jesus returns, he will return as many Jews expected Messiah to come the first time, in power and glory. When Jesus returns, he will not again submit to earthly authorities and meekly receive evil at their hands. He has suffered all he must suffer, and will return to mete out justice to the evil, and mercy to all who will receive it in love for him. The crooked will be made straight, as the Jewish prophet Isaiah foretold hundreds of years before Jesus' birth, and every human being will see the unmistakeable presence and power of God as Jesus makes everything right once for all. The Bible's final answer to the problem of evil is that evil will be destroyed. Satan and all his angels, the human enemies of God, and all that militates against shalom will be rehabilitated or removed. This "making right" is the Bible's sense of "judgment": not merely pronouncing upon what's good and what's bad, but actually correcting the bad and confirming the good.

Only in this context does the mysterious idea of hell makes any sense. Contemporary comic strips, as well as traditional religious art, picture hell as a place where demons run amok, gleefully torturing hapless human souls. But hell is not the headquarters of evil, not the palace of Satan. The Bible uses a variety of images and warnings to express a simple idea: hell is the end result of moral evil. Hell is the destination toward which moral agents, human beings or angels, take a step each time they choose evil over good. God has given some creatures free will and has promised to protect the integrity of that will by honoring its decisions. No one goes to hell who has not freely chosen it in a lifetime of deliberate action, walking a self-chosen path of independence away from submission to God and the blessing of the divine plan of salvation. As Dorothy Sayers puts it, "Sin (moral evil) is the deliberate choice of the not-God. . . . Damnation, or hell, is the permanent choice of the not-God."[24]

Hell is as removed from God as one can be. Thus the images in the Bible (and the Qur'ān) that contrast hell with heaven: darkness rather than light, pain rather than pleasure, anguish rather than joy. Hell is not a torture chamber to which some sadistic deity consigns well-meaning, if perhaps misguided, people. Hell is the logical and inexorable outcome of the careers of freely willing sinners, to which a regretful God allows them to go.

C. S. Lewis confronted questioners thus:

> In the long run the answer to all those who object to the doctrine of hell is itself a question: "What are you asking God to do?" To wipe out their past sins and, at all costs, to give them a fresh start, smoothing every difficulty and offering every miraculous help? But He has done so, on Calvary. To forgive them? They will not be forgiven. To leave them alone? Alas, I am afraid that is what He does.[25]

Is hell a condition of conscious, eternal torment? Many theists think so. Others disagree: "Put bluntly, it couldn't possibly be in anyone's long-term best interest to be eternally damned, so a loving God wouldn't damn anyone eternally. It would be more loving to annihilate people than to make them miserable for all eternity."[26] So some Christians have held that hell is the ultimate extinguishing of evil, including evil persons.

Clearly, the answer to this question lies well outside our current knowledge, so while we speculate we must not lose sight of the central point. It is this: hell is where God gives up—literally gives up creatures to their chosen end. Hell is the affirmation by traditional Christian theology that some evil cannot be reclaimed, that some losses can never be recouped, that some evil remains just evil.[27]

What about other living things, the plants and animals of the earth? What about their suffering, through predation and starvation and earthquake and flood? This remains an especially murky area for me, as the following nest of questions shows: how do we know if and how animals or plants suffer? Is the clubbing of seals different from the mowing of grass? What if we consider not only wolves savaging a deer, but stronger trees killing off weaker trees in competition for sunlight, soil, and water? Is a human hunter who kills and eats a wild boar morally different from a farmer who kills and eats a potato? Do plants or animals have any sort of "afterlife," any "compensation" for "suffering" in this world? Do such concepts even make sense for plants or animals?

The Bible hints that the natural world, as it is now, does not correspond either to its original state at the time of creation or to what its final state will be in God's re-creation. Here and there the Bible indicates that nature has somehow been implicated in the primordial moral Fall of human beings and that the natural order has been corrupted as a result (see Romans 8:19–23). Other Scriptures point to a future restructuring of the natural world in which the "wolf will lie down with the lamb," and predation will disappear (Isaiah 11:6–9).

But this is all very mysterious. How can moral decisions by human beings possibly have biological implications for other creatures? How could carnivores survive without meat? How could our entire food chain continue without some beings consuming others? And if God used evolution to create the inhabitants of our world, as many theists believe, then are we to see predation, parasitism, and all sorts of other (to us, repellent) evolutionary "strategies" or "mechanisms" as perversions of an unimaginably different evolutionary process that earlier got along nicely without them?

I take some comfort from the judgment of contemporary philosopher Stafford Betty who, having reviewed the various options offered by previous thinkers, concludes: "The approach taken by the great majority of ordinary Christians and by many of the most thoughtful Christian theologians when asked why animals suffer is to say they don't know. . . . For many this admission of ignorance will always seem the wisest, most honorable answer to give." Still, Betty goes on, "It is not the answer . . . that pleases the philosopher."[28] Nor will it please others, either. So while I cannot answer this question even to my own satisfaction, let alone anyone else's, let me put my few cards on the table.

First, the Bible tells us very little about animals and plants, and much about human beings. Most religious traditions are the same in this respect: human beings are properly the focus of human attention, and the rest of nature is mostly a backdrop to the human drama. So religious thought, and more particularly Christian thought, has little to go on in this area. Second, God created the natural world and pronounced it all "good" (Genesis 1). The references in Biblical poetry to nature are also almost all positive or at least neutral: nature is something God continues to supervise and care about. Third, if God can be trusted to deal rightly with human beings, presumably God can be trusted to look after the other beings in creation as well—not least through human care for them. Fourth, the Bible says clearly that God gave both plants and animals to human beings for food. No similar clear teaching, though, is given to us regarding the relationships of plants and animals to each other. Fifth, as noted, the Bible hints that the relationship of animals to each other and to human beings once was more harmonious (as in the Garden of Eden), and someday will be again (in the Kingdom of Christ). In the meanwhile, plants and animals share the planet with us, for better and for worse, as fellow creatures subject still to human dominion. More than this, I cannot say.

Judgment Day begins, then, the Consummation of all God's good plans for all creation. Once evil is destroyed, and once God's own have been transformed inside and out into beings fit for enjoying this new era, then God will create a new heaven and a new earth for those God has loved so long and so well. A garden city, the "New Jerusalem," is the destiny of God's creation. This Story comes to its conclusion, and the everlasting Sequel begins.

"In any discussion of disappointment with God," Philip Yancey writes, "heaven is the last word, the most important word of all."[29] In heaven, those who suffer will be comforted and healed. The alienated will be reconciled. The ugly will be transformed into the beautiful, the weak strengthened into the powerful, the dull-witted set on fire with intelligence. The lonely will be loved, and the separated will be reunited forever. Best of all, God will not be hidden any longer, and will be feared no more.

Heaven is what we actually long for when we race after money or sex or entertainment or comfort or security or love. If anything, we settle for pitifully small prizes compared with the glories God has in mind for us. C. S. Lewis put it unforgettably:

> Indeed, if we consider the unblushing promises of reward and the staggering nature of the rewards promised in the Gospels, it would seem that Our Lord finds our desires, not too strong, but too weak. We are half-hearted creatures, fooling about with drink and sex and ambition when infinite joy is offered us, like an ignorant child who wants to go on making mud pies in a slum because he cannot imagine what is meant by the offer of a holiday at the sea. We are far too easily pleased.[30]

Let us not, then, criticize the Christian story by looking at the world only from the perspective of the middle of the narrative. From this vantage point, admittedly, things look bleak and absurd. We owe it to the story and to ourselves to see where the cosmos has come from and especially where it is going before we make up our minds.

Having surveyed the story, therefore, let us turn to what reasons there may be to take the story as possibly *true*, rather than mere wishful thinking. To be sure, few of these warrants are true only of the Christian religion. Other religions make similar claims in many respects, and the question of those alternatives will be considered directly at the end of this discussion. For now, it would be well simply to consider what warrants are typically offered by thoughtful Christians for the faith they profess.

Christianity Feels Good

I admit that this heading seems trivial. After all, eating ice cream feels good, watching one's favorite television program feels good, lying down for a nap feels good. How can one use such language appropriately to describe a whole religion? One can, if one makes two points.

The first point is that Christians do claim that Christianity—like all religions—includes an affective dimension. It does make a difference in how one feels. And the Christian faith does so in several respects. Last things first: as we will consider again at the end of this chapter, Christianity provides meaning. It frames out all of life. The point here is that most of us, at least, feel good when we have a sense of location and direction, are oriented toward an important goal, and participating in an important project. And no project could be greater than working with God in the re-creation of shalom in the world. This vision, in fact, embraces all the noble efforts of all people, Christian or not.

Christianity therefore provides hope. Particularly in the face of confusion, resistance, and even the apparent defeat of our best efforts and highest aspirations, Jesus promises that good will triumph over evil; that our struggles are not in vain; that despite appearances we truly *are* progressing toward a certain outcome, the triumph of the kingdom of God on earth. It is worth getting up in the morning. It is worth each day's labor, whether marked by setbacks or successes. We walk and work with others, step by step, increment by increment, toward the guaranteed goal of peace.

Moreover, our sense of meaning and hope is based on our feeling that we are forgiven by God for our many sins and on our sense of being welcomed into God's own family. We can look forward with joy to the future because God, at great cost, has freed us from our past.[31]

Furthermore, Christianity offers spiritual, or mystical, experiences of God. Most commonly, these experiences come both through personal prayer and through worship with other Christians. That is, sometimes we sense God directly in our spirit; other times we sense God reaching out to us through others—and particularly, although not exclusively, through fellow believers.

God seems to touch a person inside with the reality of divine presence. God provides peace where there is turmoil, comfort where there is pain, companionship where there is loneliness, joy where there is sorrow or depression. God encourages the anxious, strengthens the weak, stabilizes the flighty, mobilizes the slothful. For some, at particular times, God seems almost palpable, as when people report feeling held in God's warm, strong arms (sometimes paternal, some-

times maternal, sometimes neither particularly). Sometimes the feeling isn't anthropomorphic, but metaphorical in other ways: like the
pouring into the heart of warm, shining honey. Sometimes, as Jewish
prophets reported, God's Spirit is a fire in the bones. A few people
have visions, a few hear a voice, a few feel seized by a kinetic excitement, and they dance or shout or collapse and tremble on the floor.
Depending on one's personality, need, and occasion, God's spiritual
wind will blow differently through the aeolian harp of one's soul. But
the Spirit does blow through all who open themselves to it. Christianity is not just about believing this and doing that. It is about the whole
person, and thus deeply involves the affective dimension of our being
as well.

The second main point to be made about Christianity feeling
good is that it feels right, sound, healthy, moral, affirmative of good,
and opposed to evil. True, people throughout history have committed
sins, some of them heinous, in the name of the Christian religion.
Crusaders and Inquisitors, yes, but also some pastors and parents—
the list of villains can be long indeed. But such people, it must be
allowed, are condemned by the very faith they purport to serve. For
the Christian religion forbids the slaughter of others simply because
they do not believe as we do. Authentic Christianity has nothing to do
with torture or abuse, nothing to do with subjugation and exploitation. Christians, alas, have been as evil as anyone else. But they stand
under the verdict of their own religion and will one day lower their
eyes under the steady gaze of their ostensible Lord, Jesus Christ. For
who will identify Jesus of Nazareth with these horrors? Who will
trace these evils back to his teaching and example?

In our time, we must acknowledge, troubles persist. Evil—both in
directed malevolence and in confused stupidity and pride—still
bedevils the Christian Church. The serious inquirer does well to look
past the depressing failures and consider the faith in its guiding documents and in those who exemplify the faith best, and judge it from
there. (This is simply to do what one ought to do if one were looking
into Zen Buddhism, or Native American religions, or Marxism.)

The quality of Christian faith under discussion here—what one might call its moral fitness—cannot be argued for as if there were some clear, objective, and universal morality upon which everyone agreed and against which we could measure each religion. The study of comparative religion, especially in a postmodern situation, shows us that no such crystalline consensus exists. Rather, what can be done is to set out Christianity as plainly as possible for each person to inspect.

Ironically, we cannot judge the moral fitness of Christianity (or any other ethic) without also judging ourselves. What kind of a morality do we *want*? What kind of a world do we want to work toward? What kind of a deity do we want to serve?

Christianity Works

For something to "work," it must do what it is intended to do. We may or may not approve of what it does, but that is a different issue. Under this head, we ought to consider what Christianity claims to accomplish and what it seems to have in fact accomplished.

First, Jesus claimed to forgive sin—a claim that understandably shocked many of his hearers. To forgive sins against yourself is one thing; to absolve sins committed against others is quite another. His followers later claimed that putting one's faith in Jesus would initiate a new level of acquaintance with God and place one on a path of spiritual transformation that would culminate in eternal life with God. Clearly the first claim cannot be put to any empirical test at hand: how can we know who is or is not forgiven? Nor can the last claim about heaven be tested at present. Christians do testify that they *feel* forgiven, that the burden of their past failures falls off their backs and rolls away, and that they believe God grants them a fresh start on their life journey toward wholeness.

Such a feeling is not to be despised, for who with keen conscience does not long for the relief of forgiveness? But two questions must be raised about this feeling. First, claiming to feel forgiven says nothing about the objective reality of whether or not someone is forgiven. Second, forgiveness cannot be granted by just anyone. A priest can stand up and pronounce absolution in a church service, but who is he or she to do so? Only the one offended against can forgive. Since sin in the theistic understanding is ultimately offense against God, only God (or God's representative, which is the role priests assume when they pronounce absolution) can forgive it. To resolve the objective question, we would need warrants that point to Jesus as the God who is entitled to forgive sins. For the present, we can note that Christians do experience forgiveness, as their religion says they will, and so Christianity works at least on this experiential level. (Christians also share forgiveness with others: a responsibility pledged in the Lord's Prayer itself. This is an obvious—and demanding—form of experiential validation of the Christian religion: do Christians themselves forgive?[32])

Moreover, Christianity promises power for ongoing spiritual development, and the universal testimony of Christians is that they do receive help toward personal maturity: through the moral guidance of the Church, through the inspiration and instruction of the Bible, through the transforming experience of prayer, and so on. Acquaintances of Christian converts often remark as well on the life-changing, life-improving effects of embracing Christianity. So not only in its teachings, but also in the experience of practicing those teachings, Christianity offers moral power.

Readers who know professing Christians whose lives seem less than admirable will balk at this claim. "They're no different than I am," one might assert, "and some of them are worse!" Three observations may be useful here.

First, Christianity does not claim to make people instantly perfect, only progressively better. God reaches individuals at a particular point in their lives, rescues them from spiritual death, and sets them on the path to purity and health. Some people start much further back than others, so that compared with some other people in absolute terms they seem poor advertisements for the transforming power of the Christian faith. But *relative to their circumstances*, they may be making dramatic progress.

Second, Christianity is about God working with human beings, not dolls or robots. Christians continue to have a will that can resist God, can retard development, can retain bad habits of sin. It is not necessarily the fault of God or the Christian faith that Christians act badly. For it is the Christians themselves who act badly. A music teacher can hardly be blamed for a student's poor performance if the student fails to practice and heed instruction. A parent cannot be blamed for a child's misbehavior if the parent has (by some objective standard) raised the child well and yet the child chooses his or her own way of destruction. God does not turn Christians into automatons, but cooperates with them as they will allow—much, no doubt, to God's frustration and disappointment, yet as part of the divine plan to develop spiritually mature human beings.

Third, cultural dynamics continue to encourage some people to claim adherence to the Christian religion when they in fact do not adhere to it in any meaningful way. In some areas of Canada and the United States it is still economically and socially advantageous to attend church, mouth Christian platitudes, and in other respects act superficially as a believer. Larger parts of both populations have a residual memory of Christianity received from family, school, and regional or national culture. Thus people tell pollsters that they are Christians although they never attend church, do not read the Bible, rarely pray, and know virtually nothing about Christian doctrine and history. Let us recognize that someone who never worshiped in a mosque, neglected the Qur'ān, ignored the daily prayers, and knew nothing of the *sharī'a* (or path of obedience) could freely call himself a Muslim, but no one else would have to take his claim seriously. So Christianity's claim to spiritual transformation should not be assessed by the example of nominal adherents, but rather the experience of faithful practitioners.

Christianity does not claim transformation on the individual level alone, however. It also claims to integrate people into communities of love. Indeed, Jesus' own command to his first followers was to love each other so deeply and well that others would remark on this mutual affection and service as the very sign of Christian community (John 13:33, 34). If Christian churches are manifestly *not* communities of exemplary love, then Christianity is failing to deliver on its promise.

Who can deny that Christian churches frequently fail this test? Churches are often just another group of self-centered, self-promoting individuals, no different from a social club or political party— except perhaps lacking in the graces of the former and the ambitions of the latter. Still, many people who have been or currently are in crisis would deny that their churches are failing. Churches have rallied around the sick, the poor, the lonely, the discouraged. Many people have converted to the Christian faith precisely because of the love they have witnessed among Christians, as well as because of love they have received from Christians who obey the Biblical command to love their neighbors as themselves. Such stories do not make headlines, but they are not the less authentic for that.

Many Christian churches manifestly *do* fail this test of exemplary love. The reason, however, is not hard to find. The same points as were made about individuals can properly be applied here as well. First, churches are communities in process, not in perfection. This is why, in authentic churches, those of us who don't feel perfect nonetheless can feel accepted. Second, churches do not always cooperate with the leadership of the Holy Spirit. Third, not every organization that calls itself a Christian church is, in any important sense of the term, truly Christian. None of this exonerates Christians, to be sure. What it does is hold these Christians fairly to the standards of their own faith and call them to greater fidelity.

If no fidelity existed anywhere, however, or if the incidence of Christian love were merely exceptional, then the Christian religion would have to answer for this inconsistency. But is that so? Do not Christians in general, in fact, love each other? Do they instead construct and maintain communities that pursue clearly un-Christian and unloving agendas? I suspect that the answer to this question must be sought on two levels: the macroscopic (all of the churches) and microscopic (this particular church). These, however, are not the levels upon which many people consider the question. Critics draw together this anecdote and that news clipping, this personal bad experience and that rumor, and infer from this tangle a conclusion about an entire world religion.

They would do better to consider the "macro" level, of the current worldwide state and the previous two-thousand-year history of the Christian religion. Then they would be entitled to make general conclusions. On the "micro" level, they ought to enter the doors of an authentic Christian fellowship and examine the society they find within. Understanding the dynamics of such a group takes time—as any good anthropologist must have time to study any culture, particularly if the anthropologist is careful not to let her previous prejudices get in the way of disciplined analysis. In sum, surveying the history of the Christian church as a whole and closely observing a living community of sincere Christians surely offers much more to the serious inquirer than a superficial survey of this or that set of disappointments and scandals.

Christianity is supposed to accomplish other things in the world. Christians are supposed to make converts: clearly the world's largest religion has succeeded on that score, however dubious and temporary some of those conversions have been. Christians are supposed to work with God toward shalom: sometimes they have, dedicating themselves to political, economic, cultural, or racial justice. But the promises of personal transformation and the building of loving community particularly constitute the heart of the Christian promise. And on this basis, while disappointments must be acknowledged, millions of Christians around the world testify that Christianity works.

Christianity Really Happened

For several years I taught a standard survey of Western civilization. I would come to the origins of Christianity, and I would dutifully relate a simple version of the career of Jesus of Nazareth and of the ideas and practices of the early church. After teaching this course a few times, I began to dread the arrival of this particular topic. It dawned on me that a keen and persistent student could tie me in knots by asking a particular question. Mercifully, my students never saw fit to pose the question, and I escaped without ever having to face it.

Let me relate for you the awkward scenario I feared. I have just finished my presentation on early Christianity. I ask for questions and comments, and a keen and persistent student puts up her hand.

"Sir," she asks politely, "did Jesus rise from the dead?"

I reply, "Carolyn, I tried to make clear that the early church did believe and proclaim that Jesus had risen from the dead. This is a keystone belief in the whole New Testament."

Carolyn patiently continues, "Yes, I understood that. But my question is not about the beliefs of Jesus' followers. It is about Jesus himself. You have told us in this course that Julius Caesar crossed the Rubicon in 44 B.C. and by that act initiated the fall of the Roman Republic. You have told us that Jerusalem was leveled by the Romans in A.D. 70 as an act of reprisal after a Jewish uprising. When you discussed these events, you didn't say that 'Romans believed this happened' or 'Jews believed that happened,' but that these two events just plain happened. So I am asking you, *did the resurrection of Jesus actually happen?*"

I now am stuck, wriggling on the horns of a trilemma. First, if Jesus of Nazareth really did rise from the dead, then it is significantly more probable that other, less demonstrable, elements of the Christian proclamation are real as well. It is then arguable that this historical event is the most important event in world history. So how can I, as a professional historian, not venture an opinion on this?

Second, if Jesus of Nazareth did *not* rise from the dead, then the Christian religion is founded on a fundamental misunderstanding, if not a deception. Given Christianity's impact on societies around the globe, this in turn could possibly be the most important event in world history. So how can I, as a professional historian, not venture an opinion on this?

Third, suppose that I try to avoid plunging the class into religious and historical controversy, and refuse to offer my own judgment. Suppose I retreat into fair-minded agnosticism, claiming only to conclude from the available historical evidence that *Christians believed* that Jesus rose from the dead, but also that there is no way to ascertain whether or not he actually did so from our critical vantage point. I cannot escape: for from the earliest Christian sermons to those of the present,

Christianity claims that God vindicated Jesus by raising him from the dead; that our hope for resurrection in the future depends upon this resurrection in the past; and that without belief in the actual, historic resurrection of Jesus, the Christian faith falls to ashes.

The apostle Peter, in what the New Testament depicts as the first public address of the Christian church, stood up in the midst of a Jewish festival in Jerusalem, scant weeks after the execution of Jesus in that city, and boldly cried out,

> You that are Israelites, listen to what I have to say: Jesus of Nazareth, a man attested to you by God with deeds of power, wonders, and signs that God did through him among you, as you yourselves know—this man, handed over to you according to the definite plan and foreknowledge of God, you crucified and killed by the hands of those outside the law. But God raised him up, having freed him from death, because it was impossible for him to be held in its power. (Acts 2:22–24 NRSV)

Peter links Jesus with the ancient hero King David, claiming that David himself prophesied the resurrection of the Messiah (or "Christ"). Peter bangs his point home:

> This Jesus God raised up, and of that all of us are witnesses. Being therefore exalted at the right hand of God, and having received from the Father the promise of the Holy Spirit, he has poured out this that you both see and hear. For David did not ascend into the heavens, but he himself says, "The Lord [God] said to my Lord [Messiah], 'Sit at my right hand, until I make your enemies your footstool.'" Therefore let the entire house of Israel know with certainty that God has made him both Lord and Messiah, this Jesus whom you crucified. (2:32–36 NRSV)

From Peter we can turn to Paul, another great pillar of first-century Christianity. In one of his earliest extant letters to a Christian church, Paul identifies the Gospel itself with belief in the resurrection of Jesus:

Now I would remind you, brothers and sisters, of the good news that I proclaimed to you, which you in turn received, in which also you stand, through which also you are being saved, if you hold firmly to the message that I proclaimed to you—unless you have come to believe in vain. For I handed on to you as of first importance what I in turn had received: that Christ died for our sins in accordance with the scriptures, and that he was buried, and that he was raised on the third day in accordance with the scriptures, and that he appeared to Cephas [the Aramaic form of Peter], then to the twelve [disciples]. Then he appeared to more than five hundred brothers and sisters at one time, most of whom are still alive, though some have died. Then he appeared to James, then to all the apostles. Last of all, as to one untimely born, he appeared also to me. (I Corinthians 15:1–8 NRSV)

Paul goes on to deal with an erroneous teaching apparently present in the church to which he writes, namely, that there is no resurrection of the dead. Paul replies to this idea with vehemence that becomes repetitive as he won't let go of the crucial doctrine of the resurrection—both Jesus' in the past, and believers' in the future:

Now if Christ is proclaimed as raised from the dead, how can some of you say there is no resurrection of the dead? If there is no resurrection of the dead, then Christ has not been raised; and if Christ has not been raised, then our proclamation has been in vain and your faith has been in vain. We are even found to be misrepresenting God, because we testified of God that he raised Christ—whom he did not raise if it is true that the dead are not raised. For if the dead are not raised, then Christ has not been raised. If Christ has not been raised, your faith is futile and you are still in your sins. Then those also who have died in Christ have perished. If for this life only we have hoped in Christ, we are of all people most to be pitied.

But [Paul concludes] in fact Christ has been raised from
the dead. (15:12–20 NRSV)

If I, as a professor of history, can offer to my class only the judgment that the resurrection of Jesus is a belief of the early church that
cannot be judged historically one way or another, then I am asserting
that—despite Christianity's claims to be founded on the historical
event of the resurrection of Jesus—the whole Christian religion is
instead founded upon historical uncertainty. And that in itself might be
the most important single fact of world history.

So I must decide about the purported resurrection of Jesus, as
must any thoughtful person giving even a cursory glance at the Christian faith, let alone anyone undertaking a serious examination of its
warrants in the face of the enormous "counterargument" of evil. Let
us leave my nightmarish classroom, where I am skewered by Carolyn's
intellectual honesty and unsure which teaching tack to take, and move
on to consider a positive response. What warrants can Christianity
adduce for what seems to be a preposterous claim: not just that something or someone somehow resuscitated Jesus following his apparent
death (after all, don't emergency room staff do this every day?), but
that after *three days* of death, Jesus appeared to his followers not as a
candidate for a trauma unit but as the glorious conqueror of death
and harbinger of eternal life?

The question must proceed in two stages. We must know what
information Christians believe points to the possibility of a resurrection. But before examining this evidence, we must consider what our
sources are for this information, and how reliable they are.

Our main source of information about the career of Jesus is, of
course, the New Testament. Some Christian apologists point to references to the life and death of Jesus that appear in other ancient sources,
such as the Jewish historian Josephus and the Roman writer Suetonius.
But precious little can be gleaned from such sources beyond the brute
fact of Jesus' life and its termination by the Roman authorities in Judea.
Not surprisingly, the only ancient writers who took seriously the life

and death of an obscure religious leader in a backwater of the Roman Empire were those writers who believed that he was in truth the Son of God.

The gospel writers' faith, however, does not necessarily disqualify them as competent sources of information. No historian, after all, devotes time and energy to a subject that does not interest him and about which he does not form strong opinions. Herodotus and Thucydides, the classical Greek "fathers of history," show obvious biases and not-so-hidden agendas in works that we nonetheless prize for their descriptions of the ancient world. Julius Caesar was scarcely a disinterested observer of the Roman conquest of ancient France, but his *Gallic Wars* nonetheless stands as our only important account of those events, and one that historians have taken seriously *as history* for centuries. The critical question with respect to any account is not whether the writer has a particular opinion on the subject (for all writers do), but whether the writer offers reasonable and adequate evidence for his conclusions—that is, whether or not he is a dependable source.

We can see this in contemporary, everyday examples. Sports fans can give accurate accounts of games they have seen, even those involving their favorite teams. Critics can render fair-minded descriptions of works they finally like or dislike. Even sportsmen may sometimes offer a dependable account of just how big the fish was that got away. An intelligent person rightly takes the bias of the source into account in case the bias so badly distorts the account that she no longer can trust anything in it. An intelligent person does not, however, discount her sources *simply because* they are biased. After all, most people interested in a subject—*any* subject—have opinions about it that affect, but do not necessarily compromise the veracity of, their representation of it.

Now Matthew, Mark, Luke, and John—whom ancient church tradition understands to be the gospel authors—were not professional historians. According to the early traditions, they came from four different trades: Matthew was a tax collector, Luke was a physician, John was a fisherman—we don't know what Mark's trade was. Each was an amateur simply doing his best to serve the first Christians with reliable accounts of the work of Jesus. Leaving aside the question of supernatural inspiration and even whether church tradition is correct about the authorship of what are, in fact, anonymous documents, the four gospel writers worked the same way all historians work: they collected accounts, both oral and written; reflected on whatever personal experience they might have had with their subject; and set to work writing brief portraits of their Lord for their intended audiences.

But did they write reliable history? To answer this honestly, I need to risk making enemies among my professional friends by asserting that no field of literary or historical study is as rich, but also as confused, as New Testament scholarship.[33] One can find a well-credentialed scholar proclaiming virtually any thesis imaginable about this or that part of the New Testament.

A variety of reasons explain this cacophony of dissenting voices. For one thing, no text in Western civilization matters as much as the New Testament: not the Magna Charta, not the Declaration of Independence, not "$E = mc^2$." For better or worse, no text has affected our civilization like this collection of small first-century books. Furthermore, when scholars study the New Testament, ultimate things are at stake. The text itself claims to describe the most fundamental realities: God, the world, humanity, sin, salvation, heaven, hell, morality—who can study it and remain indifferent to its implications?

So although one can recognize the eruditon of many New Testament scholars past and present, in at least some cases their expertise has been put at the service of highly personal religious agendas. In the eighteenth and nineteenth centuries, in fact, pioneering scholars such as Simon and Reimarus and Wellhausen and Baur pursued their studies with openly unorthodox, even antiorthodox, concerns that skewed their work—even as each of them made important contributions to the understanding of the Bible. There is no reason to suppose that twentieth-century scholars are so different from their distinguished predecessors.

The current scholarly voices that proclaim the Gospels to be suspect as historical sources therefore must be listened to with caution—particularly since many reputable scholars think otherwise. One must neither accept unquestioningly whatever happens to be the trend of the moment in New Testament scholarship, nor dispense with the whole field entirely. A critical arm's-length stance serves one well in any area of human inquiry, and especially in one so contested as this is.[34]

I have concluded that the Gospels are at least basically reliable in their portrayals of Jesus. They vary from each other in details, even important ones, but their individual and composite portraits of the life and times of Jesus of Nazareth seem at least as reliable as any other historical sources we have about the ancient world.

Why do I think so? For one thing, there are, after all, four accounts: not one or two, as is often the case in classical sources. And these accounts agree with each other far more than they seem to disagree. It seems ridiculous to attribute this agreement to some sort of collusion among the four writers—and yet I have had people raise just this possibility in conversation. Quite apart from the silliness of a charge of massive deceit leveled against devotees of a religious master whom everyone agrees taught honesty as a supreme virtue (it would be a different thing, for instance, to suspect collusion among Nazi biographers of Hitler), the very differences among the four Gospels to which critics often point indicate that a conspiracy of agreement is highly unlikely. In other words, only a poor conspiracy would so obviously fail to iron out the many differences among the Gospels. Instead, the more sensible explanation for four different but mutually reinforcing accounts is that they are describing the same reality from four different points of view.

Furthermore, they agree with each other far more than they do with the other "gospels" written in the first and second centuries— those attributed to the apostles Thomas and Peter, for example, or the early missionary Barnabas. The early churches quickly latched onto the four Gospels that became part of the New Testament—in church after church across the Empire, as archaeology has shown—while repudiating others as fanciful, even heretical. This widespread agreement on the status of the four Gospels against their "competitors," an agreement noted by scholars of various stripes, is a phenomenon not to be lightly received—especially in the light of recent excitement over so-called Gnostic and other "gospels." The early churches ought to be treated as the best judges of which gospels got the story right. At least a few eyewitnesses to Jesus' life were still alive at the time of the writing and circulation of the Gospels, and these eyewitnesses easily and authoritatively could have refuted, and did refute, any phony accounts. Even without the validation of eyewitnesses, the fact that the Gospels were written within the lifetimes of the first generation after Jesus (that is, between A.D. 50 and 100, with the death of Jesus dated at about 30) is persuasive: the Gospels were accepted as valid by the generation that had been taught the "Jesus traditions" by the apostles themselves. The vast majority of the early churches—and we have records right back to the late first century—broadly and independently agreed that these four were authentic.

So while scholars argue over whether Luke has a particular historical reference correct or whether John is putting words into the mouth of Jesus that he never said, we might sensibly consider one thing that New Testament scholars rarely dispute. The early Christians themselves adopted these four as their basic community remembrances of the life of their Lord. The early churches prized these four accounts because, in their view, they told the truth about Jesus.[35]

Many elements of Jesus' career upon which all four gospel writers agree are also remarked upon in the still-earlier letters of the apostle Paul, which were written in the 50s and 60s, within thirty or forty years of Jesus' death. And these letters—at least the major ones such as Romans and I and II Corinthians—were also widely received early on by most churches as teaching the truth about Jesus. So we in fact have five sources, all of them written within a century of the events they purport to describe, that disagree on details but massively agree on many essential parts of the story of Jesus' life. These five sources together constitute an astonishingly rich and reliable resource base for study, especially when compared with any other records from the classical period of Greco-Roman history. If we simply apply to the New Testament documents the same tests that professional historians normally apply to other ancient accounts, we have at least as much reason to trust the Gospels as sources of historical information about Jesus as we do to trust any other writer, writing about any other subject, in the ancient Mediterranean world.

Having said all this, we still can generously grant to a skeptic all sorts of minor difficulties in the gospel accounts as we move to make the second of our major points, namely, that historical information points to the truth of the Christian claim of Jesus' resurrection. In other words, even if one takes a minimalist approach to the historicity of the gospel accounts, even if one grants for the sake of argument that the Gospels contain a large number of relatively minor inaccuracies—or even major mistakes or fabrications—one runs up against data that are attested in all four Gospels and held up as crucial, not incidental, events in the narratives. Now, grant me just two facts—two pieces of information that clearly are not in themselves miraculous. Grant me these, and see what else might reasonably follow.

The two facts are (a) an empty tomb and (b) enthusiastic disciples. After his death by crucifixion Jesus was buried in a tomb owned by a secret follower, Joseph of Arimathea. Jesus' tomb was a cave sealed with a rolling rock of some sort. The four Gospels record many, many details of Jesus' death, burial, and resurrection. For the present purpose, however, almost all of those details can be set aside as we focus on just one: the empty tomb.

Each of the four Gospels records that it was empty (save for the graveclothes left behind). Perhaps the Gospels are mistaken or dishonest about this. But why, then, when rumors of Jesus' resurrection began to circulate in ancient Jerusalem, did neither the Jewish nor the Roman authorities (neither group being friends of Jesus or his followers, as all accounts from that time indicate) simply go to the tomb and produce the body? For that matter, why didn't any skeptic simply find out where Jesus had been buried and investigate? Given the premium that such preachers as Peter were placing upon the resurrection of Jesus, surely production of his corpse would have smothered Christianity in its cradle. It seems likely that the Gospel accounts are correct in their assertion that the tomb was empty.

Perhaps Jesus' body was not in the tomb because he had revived and escaped. This explanation, however, faces considerable obstacles. First, why would the Roman executioners, skilled in their terrible craft, be mistaken about Jesus' condition and allow him to be buried alive? Second, given the tortures of the standard precrucifixion flogging of Jesus, and of the crucifixion itself, how likely is it that Jesus would be *healthier* after a number of hours in the tomb than he was before? How much more likely that, even if he had been buried alive, he would have died from exposure or loss of blood? Third, the graveclothes in which Jesus was wrapped, if they were typical of the time (and why would they not be?), would have been made of linen fiber— extraordinarily difficult to break—in which Jesus' body would have been wrapped tightly from neck to foot, with a separate cloth for the head. Even an escape artist might find such an arrangement challenging. A victim of crucifixion freeing himself from such encumbrances is an unlikely scenario.

Still, might not a barely alive Jesus have been elaborated into a later myth of resurrection? The myth would have had precious little time to form. Few scholars doubt that Jesus was crucified sometime around A.D. 30, and most agree that Paul wrote to the Corinthians about the resurrection less than thirty years later. Myths that shape whole communities usually take a lot longer than that to form, as anthropologists and historians recognize.

The idea of myth-making begs the question as to whether these disciples were likely candidates for an enterprise of this sort. It could be, of course, that the disciples engaged in a different sort of plot entirely. Perhaps they themselves purloined the dead body of Jesus precisely in order to foment the idea of resurrection and to forestall the devastating blow against their nascent movement of the corpse's discovery. A third alternative is that the disciples hallucinated and came to believe their master was alive when in fact he was dead. Whichever of the three options one selects, one must deal with the second fact to be explained: the extraordinary attitude of the disciples after Jesus' reported resurrection.

The Gospels portray almost all the disciples as cowards during Jesus' arrest, trial, and execution. Given the widespread Jewish belief of the time that a Messiah would return in divine power to destroy precisely the Gentile oppressors who were now crushing Jesus, the disciples' descent into a confusion of terror and despair is entirely understandable. The Gospels tell us only what we would expect to hear about such followers at such a time. What needs to be explained, however, is the subsequent confidence of such followers in such a terrifically unlikely story: that the leader of their little band had in fact been raised to new life by God and had empowered them to bring the good news of his victory over evil to the entire world. Zeal was one thing, perhaps commendable in a land with little hope of freedom. But ancient Jews, according to what cultural records we have, were not more credulous about such things than most of us are today. Resurrection was the hope of some, yes, but as a reality to be enjoyed only in the awaited Messianic kingdom. One lone resurrection as the divine vindication of a crucified Messiah seemed an utter contradiction in terms, and organized Judaism soon moved to stamp out any such idea. The Christians, however, persisted, and many lost careers, families, and even their lives for their faithfulness to this one message: God raised Jesus from the dead, and God will raise you, too, if you believe.

Let's be blunt: perhaps the disciples were liars and made the whole thing up. They would have to have persisted in a large and sustained conspiracy, lasting decades. Thomas Morris reflects at length upon this possibility:

This is from the beginning an exceedingly odd sort of agreement—a number of different people get together, concoct a story, and agree to lie about it, each promising not to break and tell the truth. It is crucial to their agreement that they're all liars, but how in the world can you trust liars to keep their end of an agreement? Any supposition that the apostles of Christ met after his death and entered into this sort of agreement is especially hard to swallow. Here a number of ordinary men [and women, we should add] from walks of life in which the truth mattered, who had just spent an extended period of time with a charismatic leader whom most non-

Christians recognize as one of the greatest moral teachers in history, are supposed to have met together after the death of their leader and, to further his work, agreed to tell outrageous lies about him? This is just too bizarre.[36]

Furthermore, since it is likely that at least some of the ancient traditions about their deaths are true, then some of the apostles died for what they must have known was untrue. How likely is that? At some point, surely at least one of them would have blown the whistle to save himself. Even if all of the traditions about their martyrdoms are untrue, however, what motive would the earliest Christians have for teaching such a thing? They did not attempt to seize political power by exploiting this story. There was no commercial angle to be played. They risked suffering the same terrible fate that Jesus suffered, and at the hands of the same powers. They gained only a few thousand converts for the first several decades. *Why would they lie?*

Perhaps they did not lie, but were deluded. Again, however, how likely is this possibility? As Morris cautions, "a mistake can only be so big."[37] How did the whole group become convinced of the success of a cause and a person who had apparently been an utter failure? Did they simply make up the reports of appearances of Jesus (such as those cited by Paul in the letter quoted above), or did they actually have such experiences as figments of wishful thinking? Did they all possess such powerful imaginations—imaginations, let us remain blunt, that in this case crossed over into sustained psychosis—that they believed that they had seen Jesus, talked with Jesus, and been commissioned by Jesus before his ascent to heaven? Furthermore, did they do so with apparently no dispute about these matters among the central core of followers, even as the historical records show that the early church disagreed about very many other, much less critical, matters?

It is at least logically *possible* that the whole thing was an exercise in group fabrication of an intentional or unintentional sort. Airtight proof is never obtainable in matters of history. Each student of this historical question, however, must fairly assess the various explanatory options and select the one that fits the information best. Christians are among those who believe that God really did raise Jesus from the dead, and that this event is the once-and-for-all historical guarantee of the authenticity of Jesus' lifework.

At least one more historical matter requires explanation. Why have millions of people across dozens of cultural lines, including highly trained scholars and professionals around the world, come to believe the same truths as those first-century Jews—including this truth of the resurrection of Jesus? Can they *all* be simply credulous? *All* taking refuge in wish fulfillment? *All* setting aside their critical faculties for one wild, desperate hope? Of course, one must fairly ask the same question about any other religion or philosophy that makes such an extraordinary claim. But here our focus is Christianity, and the historical question at stake is, why so many converts, of such different stripes, to such an apparently unbelievable story? Could it be that people believe it only for the irreducible reason that it, somehow, is true?

Christianity Makes Sense

There are two ways in which Christianity "makes sense." In the first place, Christianity seems to "fit" the world as we experience it, and, in the view of converts from other faiths, it does so better than other religions and philosophies.

A thing or an idea must be evaluated according to its kind and purpose. A horse can be assessed in terms of its strength for pulling, its speed for running, its intelligence for roping, and the like. An automobile can be prized for different reasons by different people: as a conveyance, as a racing machine, or as a status symbol. A chemical hypothesis is valued for its descriptive and predictive abilities: it seems more or less accurate and comprehensive. How does one therefore begin to consider a religion?

Scholars of religion define it in two different ways. The first way is perhaps the more typical. A religion is a particular system of beliefs, practices, and (for want of a better term) dispositions or passions. We normally identify such systems with such names as Judaism, Shinto, and Buddhism. Muslims, for example, hold particular ideas to be true, act in particular ways, and cultivate particular concerns and emotions. Religions thus are described in terms of what they *are*, and so this is called the *substantive* definition of religions.

The *functional* definition instead considers what religions *do*. A widely held version of this definition understands religions to speak about and give structure to the central zone of life, our fundamental beliefs and values. A religion, in this case, is whatever functions as someone's or some group's *ultimate concern* (as theologian Paul Tillich put it), the core of one's existence around which everything else is wound. Clearly Islam, Hinduism, and Daoism function in this way and are recognized as religions. But so do Marxism, secular humanism, and pragmatism. So does hedonism, status-seeking, and egomania. "He looks after that car religiously," we might say. Or we might observe, "She's a devoted fan"—using the abbreviation for "fanatic." Whatever it is that gives meaning and purpose and direction and intensity to life, whatever gets us going in the morning, whatever drives us forward, whatever consoles us in misery, whatever stands at the centers of our lives—that's religion.

When we are assessing a particular religion, therefore, we do well to consider it according to what a religion is supposed to do. How well does this or that religion serve as the center of human life? How well does it explain the world and our place in it? How well does it recognize our highest good? How accurately does it diagnose what keeps us from that good? How well does it prescribe the solution to our problems? How much help does it give us in reaching that highest good? A religion is about all of life, from the heart outward. So as we weigh various religious options, we properly ask what religion best explains it *all*? What religion helps the most and in every way? What religion fits life?

These, of course, are the hugest possible questions, requiring the hugest possible answers. The brilliant Christian writer G. K. Chesterton (1874–1936) seemed never at a loss for words. Author of many books (including biographies, theological works, thrillers, and his famous "Father Brown" mystery stories), editor of a weekly newspaper to which he was the major contributor, wide-ranging essayist, charming poet, and tireless gadfly, words flowed from Chesterton in an apparently unstoppable flood. In only one instance—this instance —did he admit that a question had (almost) dumbfounded him:

> It is very hard for a man to defend anything of which he is entirely convinced. It is comparatively easy when he is only partially convinced. He is partially convinced because he has found this or that proof of the thing, and he can expound it. But a man is not really convinced of a philosophic theory when he finds that something proves it. He is only really convinced when he finds that everything proves it. And the more converging reasons he finds pointing to this conviction, the more bewildered he is if asked suddenly to sum them up. Thus, if one asked an ordinary intelligent man, on the spur of the moment, "Why do you prefer civilization to savagery?" he would look wildly round at object after object, and would only be able to answer vaguely, "Why, there is that bookcase . . . and the coals in the coal-scuttle . . . and pianos . . . and policemen." The whole case for civilization is that the case for it is complex. It has done so many things. But that very multiplicity of proof which ought to make reply overwhelming makes reply impossible.
>
> There is, therefore, about all complete conviction a kind of huge helplessness.[38]

However difficult such a conviction may be to articulate and defend, though, millions of people believe that they have met God in Jesus Christ, and benefited immeasurably from that meeting. Millions attest that they have found the truth about God, the world, and themselves; that they walk a path that leads ultimately to perfect well-being and blesses others in the process; and that they love the right persons and things more strongly and purely each day. Mysteries remain, yes—as they do in Buddhism, atheism, or any other human attempt to understand reality. The mystery of God and evil in particular looms darkly large on every thoughtful Christian's horizon. But Christians look around and say, even in the presence of such mysteries, that life and the Christian faith correspond well. So they trust God for what they do not yet (and perhaps never will) understand.

We should note also that this trust itself is justified in the Christian way of seeing things. Given what Christians believe about God, the world, and humanity, *one would expect* a lack of human understanding about some things. And a trust in God despite this lack also seems appropriate in the light of the basic ideas of the Christian system. Millions of Christians believe with all of their hearts and lives that Christianity makes sense.[39]

Christianity makes sense in a second respect as well. Not only does the Christian religion correspond well to many people's intuitions and understandings, but Christianity provides a framework through which believers can better understand their perception of reality. Christianity "makes sense" of the world. The Christian story is a narrative in which each person can locate himself or herself in history, and can see both backward and forward for a sense of context and purpose. Christians have some sense, even if not anything like a detailed understanding, of what the world is, who they are, and where it's all headed. Good and evil, the temporary and the eternal, the physical and the spiritual, the beautiful and the ugly or merely ordinary—the Christian religion speaks to all of these dimensions of life and sets them in a coherent pattern.

More than this, Christians have an underlying conviction of the point of it all that makes sense of both our aspirations and our fears: from the nascent shalom in Eden, to corruption, through redemption, to the final fruition of lasting shalom. We long for immortality, we ache over our sins, we grieve over our losses, we mourn for the dead, we aspire to significance—all of these feelings, so deep and so upsetting that we usually acknowledge them only in life's most extreme experiences, are intimations of truth, according to the Christian faith. We may seek, and we often do seek, to fill these holes in our psyches with sex or money or friendships or power or work or family. Or we deny them, lock them away, cut them off, and destroy authentic parts of our deepest selves. "Our hearts are restless, until they find their rest in thee," Augustine prayed. Blaise Pascal recognized the "God-shaped vacuum" in every person's heart, a vacuum that sucks in everything we use to stop it and remains unfilled. Christianity says "Yes!" to our desire to live forever, "Yes!" to our recognition that we are currently unfit to live forever, "Yes!" to our need for forgiveness and restoration, "Yes!" to our permanent attachment to loved ones, "Yes!" to our ambition to count for something that lasts, "Yes!" to our fundamental feeling that we are, in fact, utterly dependent upon God and that that is right. The Bible says, "In [Jesus] every one of God's promises is a 'Yes'" (2 Corinthians 1:20). At the heart's core, Christianity makes sense.

WHAT ABOUT OTHER RELIGIONS AND PHILOSOPHIES?

Other religions and worldviews offer their own warrants, of course. Christians are not alone in having good reasons to believe. My own experience and academic training, however, concentrate on the Christian religion, so I cannot offer a similar case for another point of view. In this respect I simply follow in the path trod first by the early Christians. Few of them attempted to demonstrate Christianity's superiority over this or that religious or philosophical option in the ideological marketplace of the Roman Empire. Instead, they said what they knew, what they themselves had experienced and thought about. And then they invited their friends, their family members, and any other listeners to consider the news about Jesus Christ for themselves.

I will point out, however, two key considerations for anyone comparing the case for Christianity with the warrants for other religions or philosophies. First, no other world religion makes the same claim regarding history. Not even Judaism does, as deeply rooted as it is in the historical event of the Exodus. The Christian faith depends completely upon whether or not Jesus of Nazareth really did die, really did rise from the dead, and really did ascend into heaven as the world's Savior. The situation is as radical as this: If someone could somehow produce the bones of Jesus today and give good evidence for identifying them as such, classical Christianity would collapse with a single blow. If one could similarly demonstrate the historical uselessness of the Gospels, particularly in their claims about the suffering, death, resurrection, and ascension of Jesus (and many people have attempted to do so, especially in the last two hundred years), then some sort of religion might remain, and it might be called "Christianity," but it would not be anything close to the faith of the historic church.

Buddhism offers its answer to the world's problems whether or not the stories told about the career of the Buddha are literally true—indeed, whether or not a historic character Siddhārtha who achieved Enlightenment ever existed. The point of Buddhism (the mainstream Therāvadin and Mahāyāna varieties) is whether it *works* to eliminate suffering. The same is true in Hinduism regarding the myths about Rāma or Krishna or Śiva: these stories are not meant to be taken as historical accounts, even if some devotees do take them as such, but as illustrations of ultimate reality. Confucian wisdom is wise on its own merits, not on the authority of an ancient Chinese sage named Kong-zi. Daoism rests on the writings of a figure, Lao-zi, who is widely judged to be mythical, and this judgment about Lao-zi is made without any cost to the vitality of Daoism—and so on, throughout the world's faiths. Even in Islam what finally matters is the authenticity of the Qur'ān as the speech of God, as instructive as are stories of the Prophet's life. Yes, the pattern of Muḥammad's life established the pattern for all Muslim devotion (and thus details sometimes do matter a good deal), but Islam does not rest as Christianity does on a miracle that is open to historical investigation. It rests on the revelation of God privately to an individual.

This distinction does not make Christianity immediately more true or admirable or sensible than other religions, to be sure. Perhaps, despite all of the foregoing argument, Christianity's claim to historicity can be shown to be false, or at least so dubious as to be worthless. The point here simply is that Christianity's focus upon particular events in the life of a particular individual does offer the inquirer unique grounds—and perhaps relatively stronger grounds—upon which to consider its particular claims.

The second consideration has emerged before, but deserves reiteration here. Religions and philosophies say different things and offer different things. They do not all offer the same God or gods—or any deity at all. They do not all offer the same views of good and evil, the same appraisal of the human condition, the same answers to human questions, and the same solutions to human problems. In short, they tell different stories, make different claims, and offer different promises. Similar as some religions and philosophies undoubtedly are to some others in some respects, they are not reducible (as many people suppose) to a "lowest common denominator" religion—they disagree too deeply about too much. Nor is it obvious how some great synthesis could bring their "best" elements together (as many others propose) without compromising their essential characters and without those "best" elements being in fact no more than a mirror of the individual synthesizer's own preferences. The thoughtful inquirer, therefore, will consider carefully just what is being offered in each case, and how well that option's views and promises square with his or her own experiences and convictions about reality. Is this religion or philosophy, one might ask, a move toward greater understanding, better character, and a desirable end? Or is it only partly right and yet importantly deficient as well? What other choice might do better?

For one example (and I select a great religion, worthy of serious consideration), I personally hope that Theravādin Buddhism is wrong. I hope it is wrong because I don't like what it says, does, and offers. I don't want it to be true that the best a human being can hope for is a complete riddance of all passion, all excitement, all emotion, all attachment in order to achieve the untroubled—because unfeeling and uncaring—detachment of nirvāṇa. Buddhism of this kind sounds too much to me like what Peter Kreeft calls "spiritual euthanasia," killing the patient (the self) in order to cure the disease (suffering).[40] I admire a faithful Buddhist's discipline, but I fervently hope she is mistaken.

In the same way, I hope that the Greeks and Romans were wrong about the nature of divinity, because I hope that the divine is not a capricious and fallible classical pantheon. I hope Advaita Hinduism is wrong because I hope ultimate reality is not an impersonal ocean of being.

Instead, I hope that Christianity is basically true—despite all the faults and mysteries and strangenesses of that religion in its historical development—because *Christianity alone offers me Jesus as Savior and Lord*. Christianity alone offers me the glorious, enigmatic, loving, and triumphant figure of the New Testament, the person I believe I have met and gotten to know over the years of my life especially through the Bible, the Church, and prayer. Christians in various traditions would experience and phrase this point differently, but allegiance to Jesus has been the basis for every decision the Christian makes, and he is the one hope we have for the future. I don't want to give up Jesus. And I don't want you to miss him, either.

Other religions and philosophies offer their own considerable benefits. A Christian can fairmindedly appreciate and honor many of these, and recognize that other religions provide their own reasons for preferring their paths to the Christian one. Having done so, though, the Christian turns back to the inquirer and simply says, "May I introduce you to Jesus?"

CHAPTER SEVEN

Thinking and Living

MANY OF US COME TO THE QUESTION OF God and evil and pose it in stark terms: *Why?* This book hasn't answered that question as we might like.

We want to know why the person we love has become sick. We want to know why the person we trusted has betrayed us. We want to know why wars rage on, why earthquakes and hurricanes keep destroying, why diseases devastate, why criminals succeed. We want to know why we cannot rid our own hearts of evil: evil ideas, evil memories, evil desires.

To ask why is to be human. We need meaning; we want to understand. It somehow helps for things to make sense, even if the sense they make is awful. So intelligent and sensitive people in all cultures and all ages have observed and felt and pondered and talked and written all they could about evil and about whatever divinity or divinities there could be. They have searched for whatever order out of chaos and goodness out of badness there could be, seeking some explanation to help them in their suffering.

Chapter 5 attempted one kind of answer, a partial theodicy that presented our world as the right sort of world for our actual condition: a world that shows us our need, and provides opportunities to grow up into personal maturity. Chapter 6 recognized the limitations, however, of this or any other attempt at theodicy. Then it went further to provide warrants for trust in Jesus Christ as the main basis for faith in God in spite of God's apparent complicity in evil. What these two chapters did not offer, however, was *certain proof* of the truth of the Christian understanding of God and evil. This book does not promise airtight, inescapable arguments that will convince any intelligent person of goodwill. Why not? It does not do so because of my conviction that *no* human explanation of *anything* can provide certainty of this absolute sort: human beings are not capable of knowing anything for certain. But it also does not do so because I believe it would be spiritually *disadvantageous* for us to have absolute proofs of such things, even if they were to be had.

HYPOTHETICAL THINKING AND GRADUATED ASSENT

We encounter evil in particular instances. We never face "war" or "cancer" or "hardship," but always *this* conflict, *that* tumor, *this* layoff. From these particular instances, we may then generalize: "Why are there conflicts?" "Why are there diseases?" "Why are there setbacks?"

When we try to answer questions about evil, our answers can stay particular.

Q: "Why did he smash up his car?"
A: "Because he drove at 100 through a curve marked for 60."

Q: "Why did she get emphysema?"
A: "Because she smoked two packs a day from the time she was fourteen."

Q: "Why did they go bankrupt?"
A: "Because they maxed-out their credit cards and couldn't make the payments."

Q: "Why is this farmland becoming less and less productive?"
A: "Because farmers have used fertilizers, plowed erosive patterns, and planted crops that progressively ruin the soil."

Yet these answers only satisfy the questioner if he shares with the answerer a great number of assumptions about the world. That is, each of these answers assumes a particular understanding of the way the universe works: of physics (tires will not adhere to pavement if the forces of contrary momentum are too great); of biology (smoking causes various diseases, including emphysema); of economics (spending more than you take in leads to bankruptcy); and of agriculture (bad farming eventuates in poor soil).

Consider the case of an inquisitive child.

"Why is the sky blue?"

"Well, it's not really blue: it just looks that way."

"But why does that happen?"

"Because of the way the sun's light bounces off dust contained in water vapor in the atmosphere." (This is a precocious child and an energetic parent.)

"But the sun isn't blue! So why does that happen?"

"The sun's light is actually composed of a full spectrum of colors, and yet it is only the blue end that reflects to our eyes, thus giving us the impression that the sky is blue."

"But why does that happen?"

"Run along now, dear, and stop bothering Mommy. Mommy doesn't remember any more about the optics of the atmosphere!"

In fairness to Mommy, her child could keep asking "why" until even Stephen Hawking ran out of answers, because a long-enough string of "why" questions leads us back to our most foundational conceptions of the universe: "Why is there light?" "Why are we here to see it?" An answer "works" only within a set of assumptions about the subject in question, each of which could well be examined for its own warrants. And there is considerable question in the most advanced theoretical reaches of philosophy and science as to whether we can actually know *anything* for certain. Instead, we have "hypotheses"—intelligent guesses as to how things might be—which we then "try out" on the world and assess for "fit." Each of these guesses in its turn is part of a larger structure of hypotheses that is itself a large hypothesis to be "tried out" on the world. At the most comprehensive level we encounter worldviews or religions or philosophies that attempt to explain everything, and we must see that they, too, are hypotheses—intelligent guesses—that are always subject to further "tryouts" to see how they fit our experience of the world.

Some important points must be considered about this way of seeing human inquiry and knowledge. We are wise to recognize (perhaps more than we customarily do) that all human thought is conducted in this way. We encounter a situation; we compose our best guess as to how to understand it (based on our prior knowledge and our assumptions about the way the world works); and then we see how well our guess (our hypothesis) works in that situation. We later encounter a similar situation, apply our hypothesis, and see how it works. If it works perfectly, we are pleased. If it works pretty well but doesn't quite fit the new circumstances, we tinker with the hypothesis and improve it—or perhaps we just store away this oddity for future consideration. If it works badly, we consider whether the new situation really is similar to the previous one. Maybe the hypothesis is still just fine, and we need instead another hypothesis to suit a different challenge. But perhaps we conclude that this new situation really is like the previous one and yet the hypothesis doesn't work satisfactorily. So we consider a radical change in our hypothesis, or abandon it for a new one.

No human being in any situation has perfectly certain knowledge. Human knowledge is like human beings: finite and fallen. First, our knowledge is finite: we normally do not know all of the information relevant to an intellectual problem; even if we did, we could not know for sure that we had acquired all such information (maybe some of it lurks just out of sight in a location we haven't thought to investigate); we sometimes do not infallibly interpret the data (sometimes we compute the measurements incorrectly or hit the wrong keys on the calculator); and even if we normally do, we could not know for sure that we had infallibly interpreted the evidence this time (maybe we were drowsy; maybe someone slipped a hallucinogenic drug into our morning coffee; maybe we have a reason-diminishing brain tumor). Contemporary analytical philosophy is embroiled in such issues.[1] Nonspecialists probably can settle for the commonsense conclusion that nobody knows everything, and that our best ideas are our best guesses—not certain knowledge.

Second, human beings are fallen as well as finite. Christians believe that the Fall affected our ability to think, as well as our ability and inclination to make moral choices. Whether we believe in a "Fall" or not, however, most of us would agree that our morality affects our cognition. We tend to see what we want to see and to believe what we want to believe. Even scientists do this: after all, if you've spent most of your adult life believing that X is the case, and your own research program is built on the belief that X is the case, and your career success depends on continuing to show that X is the case, then you clearly have a compelling interest to continue to find that X is the case.

Now, reality has a way of undermining certain beliefs about the world. People don't believe just any old thing and then hold to that belief in the face of all contrary evidence. But some of our beliefs show remarkable resistance to change if they have served us well. (How often, for instance, do we really think and act as if the world is round and not flat?) And this is true for beliefs that don't just "work" intellectually, but "work" in what we perceive to be our interests as well: our race or nation or region or city or university or company or department is better than theirs, and *voilà*, here's the "proof."

So we see that no one knows everything, and no one knows anything for certain and with perfect clarity. It is at least theoretically possible, in fact, that we are mistaken about even the most obvious things.

Yet there are many propositions and experiences about which we are virtually certain. "Two plus two equals four," we might assert with considerable assurance. "I am now looking at a book," we might affirm with (almost as much? greater?) vigor. On other propositions and experiences, we have absolutely no confidence. "$2 + 2 = 5$," for instance, or "I am now looking at a book that is playing the piano."

In between these extremes exists a range of propositions and experiences about which we have more or less confidence. "The square of the hypotenuse in a right-angled triangle is equal to the sum of the squares of the other two sides" seems to nonmathematicians to sound like the so-called Pythagorean theorem, and we were always taught that it is true, and we might even have measured a couple of triangles to make sure. But unless we have undertaken considerable and informed investigation into the matter, we probably wouldn't affirm this theorem with the same intensity with which we would affirm other items of mathematical knowledge, such as "2 + 2 = 4." And about still other propositions of mathematics and logic, say, "The square root of 456,891 is 297," we might have no immediate opinion at all.

What is true of propositions is also true of experiences. I am pretty sure I'm looking at a computer screen right now as I type these words. I am pretty sure I am *not* looking at an Academy Award-winning movie, *The Computer Screen*. In between these two convictions, however, are others about which I am not so sure. I think I hear the murmur of the building's ventilation system, but it could also be the sound of construction on campus a distance away, or the muffled roar of a jet overhead. I'd have to listen for a few more moments to acquire more information in the hopes of settling this interesting matter more firmly. And even if I did listen awhile longer, I might still not be as sure about what I'm hearing as about what I'm seeing. (Indeed, maybe I'm just so excited about this paragraph that the blood is rushing in my ears, and I'm otherwise in a completely silent room.)

Every chemistry laboratory contains long glass tubes that stand upright on a desk and have little markings running up their heights with numbers at regular intervals. These are called "graduated cylinders," as some readers will recall with fondness from their high school chemistry days. If one takes a cylinder marked for 100 ml and drops precisely 1 ml of water into it, is the cylinder now "wet" or "dry"? A person who thinks only in black-and-white terms might be stumped by this apparently unresolvable conundrum. "It's wet! No, it's dry! But, but, it's wet!" A more sophisticated person will realize that the question itself is badly put. The cylinder is neither "wet" nor "dry" per se, but contains 1 ml of liquid in an otherwise dry space.

We, too, need to "graduate" our *assent* to ideas we encounter. We need, perhaps more self-consciously than we do, to measure out our agreement in strict proportion to the warrants we have for such agreement. If my mother tells me that she loves me, I believe her statement because I have a lifetime of warrants for that proposition. If my mother offers an opinion about astrophysics based on something she watched on a daytime talk show, I will accord her statement less than full credibility. And my mother, being a reasonable person, will not take offense at my action in this case. So we need to qualify our assent to things in our own minds and in our speech. Other people should not have to ask us, "How sure are you about that?" because we ought to have told them already on any subject in which this qualification would matter. We ought to volunteer just how confident we are—and perhaps precisely what that confidence is based on—that these directions will get you to the next town, or that this wrench is just right for the job, or that our coworker really is scheming to steal your proposal, or that the best way to discipline children is to make them watch TV. And we should be aware for our own sakes of just how much doubt we really do have, or at least *ought* to have, especially about the ideas that shape our lives. Finally, we ought to investigate particularly the basic ideas (the hypotheses) we have about ourselves, about the world, and about God or the gods, and what warrants we have for those beliefs. Perhaps an alternative set of beliefs offers greater warrants, and we should consider them seriously.

Some comparisons of alternatives, however, prove easier or, at least, more straightforward than other comparisons. As long as the criteria are clear, comparisons *within* an overarching model are easy enough. A quarter-mile drag race nicely answers the question, "Which is the better car?" as long as short-distance, straight-line acceleration is the only criterion for "better" and "worse." Some people, however, value an automobile for how it corners, or how comfortable it is for long trips with children, or how economically it consumes fuel—qualities not characteristically prized in dragsters. "Which is the better person?" can be resolved by hand-to-hand combat in some instances, or head-to-head examinations in others. If one seeks a spouse, however, martial arts will be less important, normally, than marital skills. If one seeks a linebacker, grade point averages may not decide the issue all on their own.

What if one is trying to compare *religions*? (I include comprehensive philosophies and other worldviews in this category.) Religions, after all, are deeply complex things, with complicated inner workings, bewildering varieties within each species, and customs of speech and conduct that usually take years to master. How can one set about to compare them when just learning about them, just gathering adequate information, seems impossible?

Furthermore, even if one *could* gather an appropriate amount and kind of information on two or more religions, how would one decide what is in fact appropriate? On what basis would one confidently collect one sort of information (say, about basic doctrines) and set aside as relatively unimportant other data (such as the way believers dress for worship)? Isn't an implicit value judgment implied here ("beliefs are more important than clothes") that is presupposed by the inquirer: it does not "naturally" emerge from the study itself? Or perhaps it does: perhaps neither religion A nor religion B seems to take clothing as seriously as they take ideas. Yet perhaps another inquirer is deeply interested in how a religion views and treats the body, and thus sees this lack of interest in clothing as significant in this regard. Perhaps this inquirer might then judge both A and B to be deficient, and move on to the next options available for consideration.

What universal standard, therefore, can one consult in deciding among religious options? It is relatively easy to decide what an automobile is for in any particular instance and then make a decision as to which candidate fulfils that purpose best. It is less easy, but still possible, to decide what a person is for in a particular instance and adjudicate candidates accordingly. But what is a religion for? Is it to eradicate suffering? Is it to achieve individual bliss? Is it to provide social order? Is it to keep the workers docile and compliant? Is it to introduce select individuals to ultimate truth? Is it to rescue spirits from their material prisons? Is it to form a people for fellowship with a Supreme Being, leaving the rest for destruction? Who can say?

Each of us must say for ourselves, according to the wisdom we have learned and the inclinations of our hearts. As a Christian, I believe that God makes clear to people in some elementary, but important, way what really matters in life, and people choose to honor that wisdom or to elect their own alternative paths. But I have no way to *prove* that assumption. I think seeing things this way makes sense, but that's because I see things through a Christian frame, and it has worked in my life to my satisfaction. Each person must decide for herself or himself what really matters, and then try to find a way to secure it.

And thoughtful people do. They may or may not be philosophically inclined. They may or may not be spiritually interested. They may or may not be morally scrupulous. They may or may not be ethically vigorous. But they all decide what matters, and go after it. And they go after it by checking out what paths seem available to them and then following the one most likely to get them where they want to go.

So is the quest for certainty, especially about the ultimate questions of life and death, good and evil, the sacred and the secular, the eternal and the temporal—is that quest doomed? Are there no real answers, just personal preferences? Is there no way to intelligently decide?

I see a middle course. I believe, on the one hand, that human beings cannot know things for certain—how could we? But I also believe that we run up against reality every day—at least, we run up against *something* every day—and it needs explaining. Indeed, it is all that we encounter, so it's all that needs explaining. And the thoughtful person will then consider what explains it best—all of it. Yes, we see the world through models, through patterns of conscious and unconscious assumptions, impressions, and conclusions. We cannot see things purely "objectively." But we do see things, and the best we can do is to keep refining our hypotheses—however particular, however general—to make the most sense we can of what we experience.

We must not reject an option (like Hinduism or existentialism or Shinto) merely because it cannot offer us perfect knowledge. Perfect knowledge is not on offer anywhere. Our real choice is among real options, and the wise person selects the *best* of those available, and then stays alert for opportunities to refine that option or even "trade up" to a significantly better alternative.

"Making sense" of experience is not limited to "figuring things out." At a profoundly basic level, this challenge also includes making an art of life, of constructing our existence in beauty and integrity so that it is not a chaos, but makes sense.

We may think just knowing it all would be nice. But that is not an option open to us. So what are we to think, and how are we to live, instead? We are to live by faith, in faith, with faith. And what that means needs a little explanation.

KNOWLEDGE AND FAITH

In the movie *Miracle on 34th Street*, a little girl recites her mother's wisdom: "Faith is believing when common sense tells you not to." The question of the relationship of faith and knowledge shows up even more starkly in the facetious saying "Faith is believing what you know isn't true!"

Two mistakes about the concept of faith are common. The first is to think that faith is a religious word and has nothing to do with everyday life. The second is to presume that faith has no relationship to knowledge, that the two stand as utterly separate categories of assent. In fact, however, everyday life constantly presses us beyond what we know (or think we know) and requires us to exercise faith. And yet the faith it requires is intrinsically and importantly related to knowledge.

I sit on a chair in my study. I come into my study in the morning, turn on the lights, hang up my coat, and sit on my chair. A skeptic might judge this behavior excessively credulous, but I do not insist that a mechanical engineer perform a complete structural analysis of the chair each day before I use it. I recognize, if I think about it, that it is possible that today is the day the chair disintegrates like Oliver Wendell Holmes's "one-hoss shay." I recognize that during the night some disgruntled student may have broken into my office and cleverly sawn almost all the way through the chair's legs so that they will collapse immediately upon my sitting down. But upon entering my study each day, I don't normally even bring these possibilities to consciousness for rational consideration. I see my chair, I walk to it, and I plop down without a second thought—or even a first one, actually.

In this prosaic (and, one might say, *secular*) situation, I am in fact exercising faith. I am committing myself—body, if not soul—to this chair. I am not keeping weight on my feet just in case the chair gives way. I am not propping up the chair with other furniture. I don't have soft mats strewn on the floor around it. I expect the chair to stay up, and I trust it to stay up. Note also that the faith I am exercising here is not just a matter of rational belief, as in *I assent to the proposition "This chair will keep standing properly even under my weight."* I am moving beyond intellectual affirmation to a risk of action: I actually sit down on the chair. I am exercising faith, and doing so with no choirs singing or bells ringing or incense burning or priest chanting. It's just what one *does* in such instances.

This common exercise of faith, while normally unconscious, is not irrational. For one thing, I don't just sit down on any old thing and expect it to hold me up. No, I have selected precisely two pieces of furniture in my office for this sort of exercise of faith, both of them chairs. And I have good reason (or, better, *sufficient warrant*) to do so. I have a long experience of sitting in chairs, and so far only one or two have failed to support me. I rarely see anyone else fall through a chair, either, except in slapstick comedies. Moreover, I have long experience in sitting in these particular chairs, and so far, so good. Furthermore, I know a little bit about the construction of such chairs, and so I have confidence that they will continue to perform their function admirably for years to come (although I fear that the upholstered chair, bought in an auction in rural Iowa ten years ago, hasn't many of those years left). On a different tack, I believe my building to be reasonably secure against intruders at night, and I also believe that if a disgruntled student sought satisfaction from me then he would elect some means other than attacking my chair, so I don't worry about sabotage. I actually do have warrants for my faith in the chair. On the basis of what I know, I trust.

I do not know *for sure*, however, that the chair will work. For instance, the chair may contain a defect that today will finally show up in disaster. So I do not have *knowledge* about how the chair will perform moment by moment. If I am going to benefit by the chair, though, I must go beyond what I can know and venture to use it anyway. In the nature of the case, that is, I must exercise faith. Faith, then, is what we do when we cantilever our lives out over what we do not and cannot know, while anchoring our lives upon what we do know. Faith relies on knowledge, even as it moves out from knowledge into the unknown.

No one, therefore, exercises "blind faith" in anything. Everyone has a reason (even if someone else thinks it an insufficient reason) to believe what he or she believes about chairs, or scientific hypotheses, or philosophical abstractions. And this is particularly true in the most common, but also most important, of faith exercises: personal relationships.

Amy is a bright, attractive woman of thirty. She works in a government agency, and one night is invited to attend an official party. While there, she encounters Matt at the punch bowl. Their eyes meet, a conversation ensues, and soon the party disappears in the rush of their infatuation. Matt and Amy are not kids, and they know what they want in a partner. Within weeks they are engaged, with a date set six months hence. Over those six months, they spend a lot of time together. They have so much in common, and their friends agree that they make a good match. Amy grows to love Matt deeply, and he seems to love her just as much.

One Friday, though, he calls her at work to cancel their weekend plans. "I'm sorry, something's come up, and I have to work all weekend."

Amy understands: her fiancé has an important job in the diplomatic service, although she's a bit vague as to precisely what he does there.

"That's all right, honey," she replies. "I'll see you next week."

No big deal, until it happens again three weeks later. And Matt drops a passing remark that indicates that not only did he work all weekend, but his work involved a trip out of the country. Two weeks after that it happens again. A pattern seems to develop. And each time Matt—normally quite open with Amy—seems reluctant to discuss his destination or his work. Amy begins to wonder just what Matt is up to. He seems like such a good guy, and some of the things he does in his work Amy knows about and admires. But he is disturbingly secretive about other parts of his job.

This scenario sounds like the premise for some espionage or romance novel. What secret will the heroine find out about her fiancé? What will Matt do when he discovers Amy knows? Will the romance survive? And so on, and so on. The point here is that Amy is learning to trust Matt for the longest of terms. She is preparing to invest her whole life in his trustworthiness. We would judge her wise to wonder about these oddities in her future husband's behavior.

Friends would counsel her over coffee or lunch. But what ought the friends to say? "Don't trust him, find out instead all you can"— and thus build a marriage on fear? "Trust him no matter what, stand by your man"—and set yourself up for terrible disillusionment down the road? Clearly either of these alternatives is unacceptable: the former route leads to a false, hollow marriage; the second might lead to the disaster of divorce, or worse.

Amy ought to ask Matt—wouldn't we agree?—to explain himself. Then if he refused to do so, she ought to ask why he won't explain. He might tell her that his job is quite sensitive, and even that it is dangerous for her to know much about it. At this point, Amy might well decide that this isn't the life for her, and break the engagement. But she might also decide that Matt has otherwise treated her wonderfully, that they are compatible in every other respect, that the parts of his job she *has* observed seem admirable, and that she will therefore choose to live with the mystery. He has given her, she concludes, *sufficient warrants to trust him anyhow.* Someday, he promises her, although perhaps only at his retirement, she will know much more about his activities and understand why he had to conduct his life this way. But he hopes that what she does know of him already, and what she will go on to learn of him in their life together, will be enough to sustain her trust in him.

On the other hand, if Matt treats her differently—if he angrily refuses to discuss his work, or offers implausible explanations of his whereabouts on these weekends, or threatens to leave her if she won't trust him implicitly whether or not he offers her good reason to do so—then Amy's friends might well counsel her to drop this guy and move on. She ought to have good *reason* upon which to base her faith in Matt, and without sufficient reason, she is not admirable for continuing to trust him, but a fool. She does not exercise "blind faith" going into the relationship, nor does she somehow become "blind" to arguments against her faith in Matt once she is in that relationship. As an intelligent person, she remains open, at least a little, to evidence that her faith is misplaced, and when that evidence piles up, she responds. There is nothing religious about all this, of course. This is faith in ordinary life.

FAITH AS CONDITION FOR KNOWLEDGE

Faith is not merely an extrapolation or "cantilevering out" from knowledge. There are important respects in which faith in turn becomes the condition for acquiring knowledge.

Let us begin by considering a scientific laboratory. A scientist, Dr. Alpha, is attempting to convince another scientist, Dr. Beta, that she has found something important in her research. Dr. Beta is skeptical. That's perfectly all right, we should think, especially for a scientist, but poor Dr. Beta also happens to have paranoid tendencies. He has reached the conclusion that other scientists are constantly trying to trick him into believing things that are not true: he no longer trusts them.

Now, how successful will Dr. Alpha be in convincing Dr. Beta? She can show him her lab notebooks. "Fictions!" he pronounces. She shows him the computer printouts. "More fictions!" he replies. She runs a videotape of the actual experiment. "It's amazing what they can do with computer-generated graphics nowadays, isn't it?" he slyly remarks, to Dr. Alpha's mounting exasperation. She calls in technician after technician as eyewitnesses. "They're all in your pay!" he stubbornly observes.

Finally, Dr. Alpha levels what she thinks will be a crushing blow. "Then do the experiment yourself!"

"And be made a fool of?" he shoots back. "Never!" And he storms out of the lab. Dr. Beta cannot trust, so he cannot learn.

The same would be at least as dramatically true of Amy as she gets acquainted with Matt. If she presumes the worst, or even simply keeps him at a skeptical arm's length indefinitely, she will learn only a little about him, particularly if she seems obviously standoffish to him. Some initial skepticism is healthy, of course. But if Amy cannot believe anything Matt says without corroboration of, say, a legally adequate kind ("How do I know you really have the job you say you have? Can I come to the place where you say you work and interrogate the other employees?" "How can I know that you're not a pimp or a bigamist? Can I hire a private detective to watch you for the next month?"), then most of us would pronounce their relationship doomed. For Amy will never be satisfied as long as she has these extreme suspicions. She can always twist the evidence to fit her fantasies.

Worse than this, however, in the face of this suspicion Matt can, and probably will, decide not to reveal any more of himself to her. He simply walks away. He feels insulted, treated with less faith than he thinks he deserves, and wants therefore nothing more to do with this strange woman who must decide upon everything for herself. That's what happens in personal relationships. The "investigated" party can choose whether or not to reveal more to the "investigator." And if the investigator fails to move forward in appropriate increments of faith in her new friend, she risks losing the friendship entirely under the crushing weight of her arrogant demand to know all on her own terms.

FAITH IN GOD

Faith in God is not completely different, but simply the variety of faith appropriate to its object. Just as putting faith in a chair is similar to, but also different from, putting faith in a spouse, so is putting faith in God similar to, but somewhat different from, the other two. We have different warrants for trusting a spouse than for trusting God. God is, for example, normally invisible to us, and so divine activity must be inferred from its results or believed in on the basis of reliable testimony, while spouses perform a great many actions that we can readily sense. Different stakes are involved in each relationship as well. We trust a spouse with our lives, while we trust God with our eternities.

Still, putting faith in God is very much like putting faith in a lover for a lifetime—which is why the Old and New Testaments frequently picture God's relationship to God's people in terms of engagement and marriage. For one thing, we cannot know for sure that God truly is what we currently believe God to be, just as a fiancé cannot be certain of her betrothed. So we might arrive at two crucial propositions about the quest for religious certainty: it is impossible, but it is also unnecessary. We already are accustomed to taking the greatest of relational risks in this life, whether trusting a spouse or trusting a surgeon or trusting a rescuer. And we simply must perform the same exercise of trust in religious matters as well, as human beings who recognize that we do not and cannot know all before deciding.

For another thing, though the knowledge upon which one is asked to make a decision in both marriage and religion is only partial, the commitment at issue is absolute: marriage for a lifetime, religious devotion forever. With other people—with friends, coworkers, family members, and so on—we are wise to trust people neither too much nor too little. We ought to *graduate* our faith, as well as our assent, according to the warrants available. In ultimate relationships, though, we have to make more radical decisions. Amy cannot strictly calculate what faith she can put in Matt and then act proportionately. At the stage of engagement, she cannot decide to enter marriage with Matt at 60 percent, say, and then proceed to marry him "more thoroughly" as their relationship goes along. At the altar she has to decide: "I do" or "I don't." She cannot know what Matt will be like in the future. She does not even have complete or certain knowledge of what Matt has been like in the past. She must, however, make a lifetime's commitment, all or nothing, on the basis of what she does know. She must commit herself to trusting Matt. She must exercise faith that day.

Amy, furthermore, must continue to exercise faith every succeeding day of her marriage, for she will never come to full knowledge either of her husband's character or of his activities when not in her presence. And we would normally say that she is entirely right to keep trusting Matt on the basis of her increasing knowledge of him. She should, that is, at least until the sad day, if it ever comes, when the warrants *against* her continuing to trust Matt overwhelm her faith. Strange perfume on his shirt, unknown female callers on the phone: such bits of evidence eventually add up. Then, we would normally conclude, she must change her mind, and her life, accordingly.

So we face the final question, the only question, of this book. Can I believe? Can I trust God in the face of evil? This book, and others like it, can provide at best only *intellectual* warrants. Those warrants, furthermore, can at best provide only reasonable support for faith. They cannot prove the truth of Christianity beyond a reasonable doubt since (a) some of the most basic matters to be demonstrated (such as the triune nature of God, or the resurrection of Jesus) are well beyond full explanation, let alone complete proof; and (b) other religions with different claims offer their own warrants that deserve respectful acknowledgment. No, the best one can hope for is warrant sufficient to believe.

Still, we must recognize that this is true of every other exercise of faith as well. I would be a fool to refuse to sit in a chair until its adequacy had been conclusively demonstrated. Amy would be a fool to refuse to marry Matt or anyone else until the marriage had been somehow guaranteed against disappointment. Life for us humans means risk, and the wise person is the one who does not seek certainty, but seeks instead adequate reason to believe the best alternative available.

Books like this can go on as this one does, however, to invite readers to explore *existential* and *religious* warrants for themselves. Amy doesn't just find out information about Matt and decide on that basis whether to marry him. She spends time with him and his friends and family. She experiences life with him. She touches him and lets him touch her. She seeks existential affirmation, not just intellectual information.

The religious inquirer must seek God in the forms in which God makes Godself present to us. Personal prayer and Bible reading are important, yes, and God can spiritually encounter us in both of these ways. (If you've never read the Bible this way before, try praying before you read, and ask God—even if you're not sure there is one, and you wonder if you're talking to the walls—to speak to you through it.)

More obviously, God meets us through God's people, and especially in the people known as the Body of Christ, the Church. As Amy cannot penetrate telepathically into Matt's mind, but must instead get to know him through his voice, his facial expressions, his actions—in short, the actions and features of his body—so inquirers can get to know Jesus Christ in his earthly manifestation, the Church.

I suggest to the inquiring reader, therefore, that you find a church in which people seem enthusiastic and genuine, a church that is closely allied with the spirit of Jesus (not every church is like this, alas), and talk to them. Spend time with them, and try to discern Jesus in them. Find out if they do know God in Christ, and (strange as the prospect sounds) ask them to introduce you to Jesus—in prayer, in the Eucharist, in Scripture and preaching, in the company of Christians, and in the other means God has given us to enjoy communion with God and with each other in the Church. For the promise of Christianity, the good news at its heart, is not a set of metaphysical beliefs or a code of ethics or even a community of believers—although Christianity includes all of these. The heart of Christianity is *personal*: the astonishing prospect of meeting God spiritually in one's innermost being and finding Jesus Christ reaching toward you for a loving embrace. Philosopher Linda Trinkaus Zagzebski has testified, "The experience of knowing holy people is still the most important evidence to me for the truth of Christianity."[2] Books can only point to such a reality. Then, like this one, they must be laid aside, and spiritual investigation begin.

For deciding among various understandings of God and evil is not, at last, a matter of the intellect: "Let's add up columns A, B, and C, and calculate which religious option comes out best." Indeed, one does not "choose" to believe a proposition: one is either convinced by its warrants or not—or (in the spirit of "graduated assent") we would say that one is *more or less* convinced by the warrants at hand. Deciding about faith in God, however, goes beyond analysis by the intellect to action by the will. And so it is with every human decision to trust rather than merely "conclude." One finally has to decide whether to sit in the chair. Amy has to decide whether to marry Matt. A seeker has to decide whether to commit himself or herself to God.

The fundamental human problem is not ignorance (a deficiency in the intellect) but sin (a defect in the soul). We are alienated from God, even resistant toward God. Perhaps this reality points toward the most basic reason of all that God does not satisfy our desire to know "Why?" in the presence of evil. More than explanation, we need re-formation. Our ancestors chose to act independently of the guidance of God. They wanted to be gods themselves, deciding for themselves about good and evil. And we have emulated their destructive independence ever since. Yet we were created as dependent beings. We need each other, we need the earth and its other inhabitants, and we need God—all in the beautiful complex of shalom. Perhaps, then, we must do without some of the explanations we seek precisely because we would receive them in just the way Job was prepared to receive them: as an accuser who presumed to judge God. God reminded Job most vividly of Job's dependence upon a Creator whose ways were well beyond Job's comprehension.

Philip Yancey has pointed out that the ancient Israelite nation, after its exodus from Egypt, enjoyed the direct guidance of God every day through Moses. God was right there in their midst, in the "tent of meeting," and Moses would go in to consult with God "as a man speaks with his friend." We might think we would do better if God would just become visible and speak to us audibly. Well, that was the actual experience for a whole generation of Israelites in the wilderness of Sinai. Did they therefore become especially devout?

On the contrary. They became whiny, greedy, impatient, and disobedient children who wanted God to perform *now* according to their immediate whims, or they would huffily march back to Egypt. God's immediate and evident presence was apparently no guarantee of spiritual maturity. God's proximity was not the solution. It only made more obvious the real source of trouble, the hearts of the people themselves.[3] And if we aren't convinced by this truth, we might consider how people responded when God later took human form and lived among us for several decades. No, the problem is not that God is far away. The problem is what we tend to do with God whether God is distant or near.

This painful lesson stands at the heart of our encounter with evil. We need to be struck off our self-built pedestals—or, in another mode, we need to be opened up out of our self-absorption—and then restored to a healthy, normal dependence, if we would but recognize it as such. Our condition of limitation, even confusion, in this complicated and sometimes frighteningly contradictory world can drive us away from the God who seems to make no sense, or it can drive us to trust God, and keep trusting, in the face of such threats to faith. The space-walking astronaut can finally assert his independence and cut loose from the annoying tethers that constrict his freedom, but he is "independent" and "free" to do but one thing: to die. The wise person learns his limits and how to accomplish the most he can within them, with gratitude to those things and those persons that sustain him in his efforts.

In heaven, we will have left behind the evil that bedevils us. We will have more knowledge than ever as we enjoy a face-to-face encounter with God in unimaginable clarity. So in one sense our struggle with evil in this world is not a helpful preparation for the next. It would make sense to practice advanced climbing techniques in a dark gymnasium if one were anticipating a rock climb at night, but not if one is expecting instead to walk down a level street at midday. What connects the experience of this world with the next, then, is not the struggle against evil, which will end, but the posture of faith (with its accompanying virtues) that such struggle encourages and that is fundamental to our going on to enjoy the life to come forever. We learn it now, we practice it now, for eternity. For eternity with God will not be the interminable boredom of pink clouds and lyres, but an ongoing life of cooperation with God that will make the most exciting and complex aspects of this life look dull and primitive by comparison.[4]

Only a perfectly good, perfectly powerful God can offer us the transformation we each and all so desperately need. Do we have the humility and intelligence to acknowledge that need and accept the proffered solution to it? Living is more than thinking. We must think, but then we must decide. Books and arguments can remove obstacles, clarify misunderstandings, and point the way forward. But the library of the mind is just the anteroom outside the parlor of the spirit. At some point we must get up from the desk, turn out the lamp, and walk through the next door. For in the privacy and intimacy of the parlor, we will encounter our Guest and start the only conversation that finally matters.

DECIDING AND ACTING IN SPITE OF EVIL

Jesus spent much of his public career talking. He addressed crowds, he taught his disciples, and he conversed privately with individuals of various sorts—from peasants to priests to politicians to prostitutes. So today he stands ready to speak with any who seek him out.

Life, however, is more than talk. Commitments to God, like commitments at weddings, begin with talk, but immediately proceed to other actions: walking together from the place of covenant making and out into the world of day-to-day action, the place of covenant keeping. We must leave the parlor after awhile and head for the workroom, the kitchen, the hospital, the nursery.

The Christian religion is not finally about what we think, but whom we love. And love is not finally about emotion, but action. Whatever we happen to conclude in our minds about God and evil, our lives demonstrate what we truly believe.

For one thing, our lives demonstrate whether we really care about the question of God and evil or not. Thomas Morris challenges us: "Many people who spend weeks mastering a new video game, months learning a tennis serve, or years perfecting a golf swing will not invest a few days, or even a matter of hours, in the effort to understand better some of the deeper questions about life."[5] Readers who have gotten this far can be commended for putting their interest into action. The same is truer about anyone who further investigates the argument of this book by looking seriously into the Christian religion: visiting churches, reading more books, trying out prayer, and so on. One has to love the truth to find the truth. The most important things in life rarely come to those who do not press hard after them: not music, not literature, not athletic skills, not wholesome relationships. Talk is cheap, action is costly. But some things cost a lot, and only love will justify the expense.

Our lives also demonstrate the level of our concern to respond to evil. "Why doesn't God do something?" we shout in the presence of evil. That is a question that Christianity takes seriously, as this book has taken it seriously over the preceding pages. But at last we come also to its corollary in the Christian understanding of things, the question that takes seriously our freedom and dignity as moral agents: Why don't you do something?[6]

Thinking and talking are good—essential, actually, if we are going to improve our lives and our ability to use those lives as effectively as possible in the service of others. Thinking and talking, though, must produce the fruit of compassion and justice and perseverance and gentleness and duty and art. Otherwise such thought and talk are literally sterile, lifeless, fruitless, useless. Worse, they can substitute for honest and useful activity, and so make us less useful than if we had avoided them entirely. As Henri Blocher puts it, "Evil is not there to be understood, but to be fought."[7] Jesus does not call us merely to think about things. He calls us to serve God and the world God loves, to work with God in spite of evil and in the service of everlasting good. That's the point of it all. That is shalom.

And we must begin by acknowledging that evil isn't just out there, as some external threat against which we might heroically struggle, but also *in here*, in the recesses of our own hearts. Where do we begin to crusade against evil? In our own lives. As Marilyn McCord Adams challenges us, "Continual repentance is . . . the best contribution [anyone] can make toward solving the problem of evil."[8]

What do you think about God and evil? Your life is your answer.

NOTES

Introduction

1. C. S. Lewis, *A Grief Observed* (New York: Bantam, 1976 [1961]); Martin E. Marty, *A Cry of Absence: Reflections for the Winter of the Heart* (San Francisco: Harper & Row, 1983); Luci Shaw, *God in the Dark: Through Grief and Beyond* (Grand Rapids, MI: Zondervan, 1989); Gerald L. Sittser, *A Grace Disguised: How the Soul Grows through Loss* (Grand Rapids, MI: Zondervan, 1996); Nicholas Wolterstorff, *Lament for a Son* (Grand Rapids, MI: Eerdmans, 1987). For briefer reflections, see John Claypool, "Life Is a Gift," in *Tracks of a Fellow Struggler* (Dallas, TX: Word, 1974), 67–83, reprinted in *A Chorus of Witnesses: Model Sermons for Today's Preacher*, ed. Thomas G. Long and Cornelius Plantinga Jr. (Grand Rapids, MI: Eerdmans, 1994), 120–30.

2. I am indebted here to the so-called Reformed epistemology of Alvin Plantinga, Nicholas Wolterstorff, William Alston, and others. For helpful introductions to these views, see Alvin Plantinga and Nicholas Wolterstorff, eds., *Faith and Rationality: Reason and Belief in God* (Notre Dame, IN, and London: University of Notre Dame Press, 1983); and Nicholas Wolterstorff, *Reason Within the Bounds of Religion* (Grand Rapids, MI: Eerdmans, 1979 [1976]). I refer readers interested in the epistemic validity of religious experience to William P. Alston, *Perceiving God: The Epistemology of Religious Experience* (Ithaca, NY, and London: Cornell University Press, 1991).

3. Lewis, *A Grief Observed*, 5.

Chapter One   *Is There a Problem?*

1. The quotation is from David Hume, *Dialogues concerning Natural Religion*, ed. Martin Bell (London: Penguin, 1990 [1779]), 108–109. A recent bibliography on the so-called problem of evil is Barry C. Whitney's *Theodicy: An Annotated Bibliography on the Problem of Evil 1960–1990* (New York and London: Garland, 1993).

2. For further introduction to the category of evil in various religions, see John Bowker, *Problems of Suffering in Religions of the World* (Cambridge, UK:

Cambridge University Press, 1970); William Cenkner, ed., *Evil and the Response of World Religion* (St. Paul, MN: Paragon, 1997); Ronald M. Green, "Suffering," in *Encyclopedia of Religion*, ed. Mircea Eliade (New York: Macmillan, 1987), 14:430–40; and Paul Ricoeur, "Evil," in *Encyclopedia of Religion*, ed. Mircea Eliade (New York: Macmillan, 1987), 5:199–208.

3. I have Paul Tillich in mind here especially: see his *Systematic Theology*, 3 vols. (Chicago: University of Chicago Press, 1951, 1952, 1963); and *The Courage to Be* (New Haven, CT: Yale University Press, 1952).

4. I have addressed this subject at a little greater length elsewhere: see "God as Lord and Lover: Masculine Language Revisited," *The Christian Century* 109 (11 November 1992):1020–21.

5. For a contemporary argument that God leaves much of the workings of the world up to chance, although from a more traditionally theistic perspective, see Peter van Inwagen, "The Place of Chance in a World Sustained by God," in *God, Knowledge, and Mystery: Essays in Philosophical Theology* (Ithaca, NY, and London: Cornell University Press, 1995), 42–65.

6. From the Chandogya Upanishad in *The Upanishads: Breath of the Eternal*, ed. and trans. Swami Prabhavananda and Frederick Manchester (New York: New American Library, 1957); excerpted in Roger Eastman, ed., *The Ways of Religion*, 2nd ed. (New York and Oxford: Oxford University Press, 1993), 21.

7. *Analects* VI:20; in W. T. de Bary et al., eds., *Sources of Chinese Tradition*, vol. 1 (New York: Columbia University Press, 1960), 29.

8. Gia-fu Feng and Jane English, trans., *Tao Te Ching* (London: Gower, 1972); excerpted in Eastman, ed., *The Ways of Religion*, 213.

9. The following account relies upon the *Buddhacarita* of Ashvaghosha, as rendered in *Buddhist Mahayana Texts*, Sacred Books of the East, vol. 49 (Oxford: Oxford University Press, 1894), 1–157; excerpted in *Anthology of World Scriptures*, ed. Robert E. Van Voorst (Belmont, CA: Wadsworth, 1994), 75–81.

10. A recent exposition of secular humanism, by perhaps its most active American exponent, is Paul Kurtz, *Living without Religion: Eupraxophy* (Amherst, NY: Prometheus, 1994). See also Carl Sagan, *The Demon-Haunted World: Science as a Candle in the Dark* (New York: Random House, 1995).

11. Quoted in H. S. Thayer, "Pragmatism," in *Encyclopedia of Philosophy*, ed. Paul Edwards (New York: Macmillan, 1967), 6:433.

12. The illustration is suggested in Francis A. Schaeffer, *The God Who Is There: Speaking Historic Christianity into the Twentieth Century* (London: Hodder and

Stoughton, 1968), 23. For more positive introductions to existentialism, see John Macquarrie, *Existentialism* (Harmondsworth, England: Penguin, 1972); and Roger L. Shinn, *The Existentialist Posture*, rev. ed. (New
York: Association Press, 1970).

13. We shall examine Mackie's argument more carefully in chapter 5.

Chapter Two   *What Is Evil?*

1. I realize that I am disagreeing here not only with dualists per se but also
with such eminences as Christian theologian Karl Barth, who writes
about *das Nichtige* as more than an abstraction (although Barth is
extremely difficult to understand on this point). I am aware also that the
Bible contains hints that God is struggling against chaos, even perhaps
in Genesis 1, and that some interpreters think this means that chaos is a
sort of alternative principle or stuff that resists God. But I remain
unconvinced exegetically, theologically, and philosophically that evil is
truly a something, rather than an abstraction that sums up the various
things that are wrong in the universe that God first created entirely
good.

Even if I am wrong on this point, however, it does not change the
point I want to make in the main text. Even if, that is, chaos or evil is
some primeval reality against which God struggles or with which God
works, God cannot be blamed for creating it. Thus the question "Why
did God create evil?" is still a nonstarter.

2. Cornelius Plantinga Jr., *Not the Way It's Supposed to Be: A Breviary of Sin* (Grand
Rapids, MI: Eerdmans, 1995).

3. Stephen Jay Gould, "The Panda's Thumb," in *The Panda's Thumb: More Reflections in Natural History* (New York and London: Norton, 1980), 19–26; the
quotation is from pp. 20–21. Gould here follows his master. Darwin
noted that certain squirrels apparently had learned to take ears of corn
rather than the customary nuts, an alteration in their behavior that Darwin concluded in his notebook "surely is not worthy [of the] interposi-
tion of deity" (quoted in Peter Brent, *Charles Darwin: A Man of Enlarged
Curiosity* [New York and London: Norton, 1981], 292).

4. Brent, *Charles Darwin*, 285.

5. Peter Brent quotes Darwin as testifying thus: "Disbelief crept over me at
a slow rate, but was at last complete" (p. 314). The erosion of Darwin's
Christianity is a theme in this biography, as it is in others.

6. Gould's collection in The Panda's Thumb can serve as just one of many examples; for Richard Dawkins, see especially The Blind Watchmaker: Why the Evidence of Evolution Reveals a Universe without Design (New York: Norton, 1986). See also Daniel C. Dennett, Darwin's Dangerous Idea: Evolution and the Meanings of Life (New York: Simon & Schuster, 1996). For critiques of such evolutionists, see Michael J. Behe, Darwin's Black Box: The Biochemical Challenge to Evolution (New York: Free Press, 1996); and two books by Phillip E. Johnson: Darwin On Trial (Downers Grove, IL: InterVarsity Press, 1993 [1991]); and Reason in the Balance: The Case against Naturalism in Science, Law, and Education (Downers Grove, IL: InterVarsity Press, 1995).

7. A recent taxonomy is offered in Ted Peters, Sin: Radical Evil in Soul and Society (Grand Rapids, MI: Eerdmans, 1994).

8. Plantinga, Not the Way, 22–23.

9. For classic reflections on this question, see Reinhold Niebuhr, Moral Man and Immoral Society: A Study in Ethics and Politics (New York: Charles Scribner's Sons, 1960 [1932]).

10. For an introduction to the Qur'ān's portrayal of Satan, see Fazlur Rahman, Major Themes of the Qur'ān (Minneapolis, MN, and Chicago: Biblioteca Islamica, 1980), 18, 121–31. For the Biblical view, see Michael Green, I Believe in Satan's Downfall (London: Hodder and Stoughton, 1981).

11. Psychoanalyst M. Scott Peck and historian Jeffrey Burton Russell are two significant examples of people whose study of evil has led them to believe in the existence of a devil: see M. Scott Peck, People of the Lie: The Hope for Healing Human Evil (New York: Simon & Schuster, 1983); Jeffrey Burton Russell, The Prince of Darkness: Radical Evil and the Power of Good in History (Ithaca, NY: Cornell University Press, 1988).

12. Hans Schwarz, Evil: A Historical and Theological Perspective (Minneapolis, MN: Fortress, 1995), 199.

13. David Hume, Dialogues concerning Natural Religion, ed. Martin Bell (London: Penguin, 1990 [1779]), 116–17.

14. Quentin Smith, "An Atheological Argument from Evil Natural Laws," International Journal for Philosophy of Religion 29 (1991):159–74. (I am indebted to Kirk Durston for this reference.) Probably the most-discussed essay on this theme, which also features a dying animal in a forest, is William L. Rowe, "The Problem of Evil and Some Varieties of Atheism," American Philosophical Quarterly 16 (1979):335–41.

15. I thank Brian Loewen for this observation.

16. The "yet another instance of X" phenomenon exemplified in this passage is sometimes referred to as "surplus evil," as in the formulation by Daniel T. Snyder ("Surplus Evil," *Philosophical Quarterly* 40 [January 1990]:78–86; I am indebted for this reference to John S. Feinberg, *The Many Faces of Evil: Theological Systems and the Problem of Evil* [Grand Rapids, MI: Zondervan, 1994], 184 n. 58). But for our purposes we can keep gratuitous and surplus categories together.

Chapter Three   *Further Problems*

1. Elie Wiesel, *Night*, trans. Stella Rodway (New York: Bantam, 1982 [1960]), 32.
2. For reflections on this theme, see C. S. Lewis, *The Abolition of Man: How Education Develops Man's Sense of Morality* (New York: Macmillan, 1947).
3. This is an assertion in the title essay: Albert Camus, *The Myth of Sisyphus (and Other Essays)*, trans. Justin O'Brien (London: Hamilton, 1955).
4. See Thomas V. Morris, *Making Sense of It All: Pascal and the Meaning of Life* (Grand Rapids, MI: Eerdmans, 1992), 89–90.
5. Ingmar Bergman, *Four Screenplays of Ingmar Bergman*, trans. Lars Malmstrom and David Kushner (New York: Simon & Schuster, 1960), 150; I am indebted to Luci Shaw's *God in the Dark: Through Grief and Beyond* (Grand Rapids, MI: Zondervan, 1989), 135, for reminding me of this scene.
6. I realize that I am opposing some leading minds of our century in this regard: theologians Karl Barth and Paul Tillich, who seem (in their different ways) to think that evil is entailed by existence, and psychoanalysts Carl Jung and Erich Fromm, who seem (in their different ways) to embrace evil as a necessary component of the process of becoming ultimately good. Even Augustine can be read as seeing evil as contributing to perfection. (See Hans Schwarz, *Evil: A Historical and Theological Perspective* [Minneapolis, MN: Fortress, 1995], for a helpful, if cursory, catalogue of classical and contemporary views.) To what I have said already I will simply add here that it is one thing to say that good can result from evil, and even that certain evils are necessary to produce certain goods *given our current situation*. Childbirth is unavoidably traumatic, for example, and parenting unavoidably entails hurt feelings on both sides and between parents. It is another thing to posit evil as logically necessary for good. Such an assertion runs counter to the Biblical understanding of a creation that begins entirely good; of a fall that is tragic (not "liberating,"

as per Fromm or "necessary" as per Tillich); of a process of redemption that is pictured largely in grim terms of rescue, warfare, and rehabilitation; and of the fully realized kingdom of God in which evil has no place. Chapter 6 expands on "the Christian story" in this regard.

Chapter Four   *Other Angles*

1. For this viewpoint, see John Kekes, *Facing Evil* (Princeton, NJ: Princeton University Press, 1990). Kekes's attempt to distinguish his views from relativism (pp. 234–35) and his more general attempt to construct a secular humanist morality depend entirely on the assumption that this world is all there is. Kekes believes that he, and others who share his perspective, are capable of judging that some things are objectively evil without reference to a divine order, for some things militate against what Kekes calls "the fundamental goal of morality: promoting human welfare." Quite apart from the question of whether one can indeed define, without reference to transcendent values, what "human welfare" consists of (sensual pleasure? physical security? emotional maturity? spiritual insight?), this whole project leaves aside the crucial question of whether some other welfare is in fact more worthy of our pursuit than human welfare per se, such as the welfare of the planet, or the glory of God.

2. Fyodor Dostoyevsky, *The Brothers Karamazov*, trans. David McDuff (London: Penguin, 1993 [1880]), 276.

3. Ibid., 282.

4. Ibid., 280.

5. Paul W. Brand and Philip Yancey, *Pain: The Gift Nobody Wants* (New York: HarperCollins, 1993).

6. For reflections on this theme, see Diogenes Allen, "Natural Evil and the Love of God," in *The Problem of Evil*, ed. Marilyn McCord Adams and Robert Merrihew Adams (Oxford and New York: Oxford University Press, 1992 [1990]), 189–208. Beyond Allen's own views, he helpfully points toward modern testimonies to God's presence in suffering offered by Edith Barfoot, Basilea Schlink, and Simone Weil.

7. As C. S. Lewis observed, "You can't see anything properly while your eyes are blurred with tears" (*A Grief Observed* [New York: Bantam, 1976 (1961)], 53).

8. Aldous Huxley, *Brave New World* (New York: Harper, 1950).

9. David Hume, *Dialogues concerning Natural Religion*, ed. Martin Bell (London: Penguin, 1990 [1779]), 114–15.

10. Cornelius Plantinga Jr., *Not the Way It's Supposed to Be: A Breviary of Sin* (Grand Rapids, MI: Eerdmans, 1995), 3–4.

11. Ibid., 141.

Chapter Five   *A Good World After All?*

1. For examples of such questions, see Robert M. Adams, "Must God Create the Best?" and Philip L. Quinn, "God, Moral Perfection, and Possible Worlds," in *The Problem of Evil: Selected Readings*, ed. Michael L. Peterson (Notre Dame, IN: University of Notre Dame Press, 1992), 275–88 and 289–302.

2. My thinking about *shalom* and its realization in the New Jerusalem has been aided especially by the following books: Jacques Ellul, *The Meaning of the City*, trans. Dennis Pardee (Grand Rapids, MI: Eerdmans, 1970); Richard J. Mouw, *When the Kings Come Marching In: Isaiah and the New Jerusalem* (Grand Rapids, MI: Eerdmans, 1983); and Nicholas Wolterstorff, *Until Justice and Peace Embrace* (Grand Rapids, MI: Eerdmans, 1983).

3. "Vandalism of Shalom" is the title of chapter 1 in Cornelius Plantinga Jr., *Not the Way It's Supposed to Be: A Breviary of Sin* (Grand Rapids, MI: Eerdmans, 1995).

4. C. S. Lewis, *The Problem of Pain* (New York: Collier Macmillan, 1962), 63–64.

5. J. L. Mackie, "Evil and Omnipotence," *Mind* 64 (1955):201. This essay has been reprinted several times (including in the anthology by Michael Peterson noted above). It joins a number of other distinguished modern essays in *The Problem of Evil*, ed. Marilyn McCord Adams and Robert Merrihew Adams (Oxford and New York: Oxford University Press, 1990).

6. An early version of this defense is in Alvin Plantinga, *God and Other Minds* (Ithaca, NY: Cornell University Press, 1967), 131–55. A fuller presentation was published in Alvin Plantinga, *The Nature of Necessity* (Oxford: Clarendon, 1974), 164–95. The most accessible version is in Alvin C. Plantinga, *God, Freedom and Evil* (Grand Rapids, MI: Eerdmans, 1977 [1974]), 5–64.

7. William Hasker and Michael Peterson have devoted considerable attention to such matters, particularly under the category of "gratuitous

evil." For a statement of Hasker's ideas, see his "The Necessity of Gratuitous Evil," *Faith and Philosophy* 9 (January 1992):23–44. For a thorough presentation of Peterson's ideas, see his *Evil and the Christian God* (Grand Rapids, MI: Baker, 1982).

8. It must be clarified that God is not looking forward to an actual future for beings which God is still deciding whether to create—that would be nonsense. Instead, God is using what is called "middle knowledge," the knowledge of what *would* happen if such-and-such a situation were to be the case. Whether God *has* such knowledge has been, in fact, hotly disputed among philosophers.

9. Henri Blocher, *Evil and the Cross*, trans. David G. Preston (Downers Grove, IL: InterVarsity Press, 1994 [1990]), 95.

10. Lest anyone wonder if I am misconstruing this fundamental point in Kushner's presentation, let me quote the title of its penultimate chapter: "God Can't Do Everything, But He Can Do Some Important Things" (Harold S. Kushner, *When Bad Things Happen to Good People* [New York: Avon, 1981]).

11. Plantinga, *Not the Way*, 73; Peck's book is *People of the Lie: The Hope for Healing Human Evil* (New York: Simon & Schuster, 1983).

12. Blocher, *Evil and the Cross*, ch. 4.

13. William Hasker, "On Regretting the Evils of This World," *Southern Journal of Philosophy* 19 (1981):425–37; reprinted in *The Problem of Evil: Selected Readings*, ed. Michael L. Peterson (Notre Dame, IN: University of Notre Dame Press, 1992), 153–67.

14. Peter Kreeft, *Making Sense Out of Suffering* (Ann Arbor, MI: Servant Books, 1986), 87.

15. Some readers will properly discern here debts both to Augustine's theodicy in *On Free Choice of the Will*, trans. Anna S. Benjamin and L. H. Hackstaff (Indianapolis: Bobbs-Merrill, 1964); and to John Hick's "soul-making" theodicy in *Evil and the God of Love* (New York: Harper & Row, 1966; rev. ed., 1978). I differ with both authors in important respects, however: for example, I am dubious about Augustine's quasi-Platonic understanding of evil as simply "privation of good," and I disagree with Hick's universalism—the belief that one day God will reconcile everyone and everything to Godself. Therefore, neither Augustine nor Hick must be blamed for my version of Free Will Theodicy!

16. Neil Postman, *Technopoly: The Surrender of Culture to Technology* (New York: Vintage Books, 1993 [1992]), 90.

17. Plantinga, *Not the Way*, xiii.

18. Ibid., 37.

19. LW 6:90f; quoted in Hans Schwarz, *Evil: A Historical and Theological Perspective*, trans. Mark W. Worthing (Minneapolis, MN: Fortress, 1995), 146.

20. Nicholas Wolterstorff, *Lament for a Son* (Grand Rapids, MI: Eerdmans, 1987), 73.

21. I don't want to press this very far, but perhaps it was a sort of "severe mercy" (C. S. Lewis's phrase) that God did *not* give my grandmother the choice. For then she would have had to shoulder an excruciating double burden every moment of the rest of her life: enduring the illness itself, plus summoning up the courage to choose to keep enduring it. It is heroic, that is, to choose to suffer on behalf of others in a crisis. To me, at least, it is unimaginably heroic for someone to choose such suffering day in and day out over years. It might be just too much to ask, and so God doesn't. Instead, God might have allowed my grandmother's illness all those years in keeping with what God knew to be her own heart's desire.

22. Joel Ostrow reflects on this theme in his poignant short story "Small Consolation," *Atlantic Monthly* 279 (April 1997):85–88.

23. Christians, of course, will see in this example a reflection of the central instance of such suffering: Christ on the cross. From a Christian point of view, the crucifixion of Jesus ranks as the most evil event in human history. Yet in context and on the whole, it was good for Jesus to undergo this suffering in order to redeem humankind. Indeed, the Bible makes it clear that God willed this event, evil as it was, precisely for this redemptive benefit. And it is the sort of suffering my grandmother underwent, I believe, as well as classic instances of Christian suffering such as martyrdom, that shed light on the mysterious words of the apostles Peter and Paul about Christians' sharing in the sufferings of Christ himself (I Peter 4:13; Phil. 3:10; Col. 1:24). For this is an essential part of what Christian discipleship means: following Christ, even at the cost of one's own life, in order to serve God's good purposes in the world.

24. B. A. Gerrish, *Grace and Gratitude: The Eucharistic Theology of John Calvin* (Minneapolis, MN: Fortress, 1993), 100.

Chapter Six   *The Fork in the Road*

1. Fyodor Dostoyevsky, *The Brothers Karamazov*, trans. David McDuff (London: Penguin, 1993 [1880]), 278.

2. Henri Blocher, *Evil and the Cross*, trans. David G. Preston (Downers Grove, IL: InterVarsity Press, 1994 [1990]), 125.

3. I once also had someone (mis-)quote John 13:7 from the King James Version as a divine promise that, in general, "what I do now ye know not, but ye shall know hereafter." Yet we must recognize that this promise occurs in the context of Jesus replying to his disciple Peter's mystification as to why Jesus was performing the rite of foot washing as a symbol of service. Thus a modern translation shows the specific (and not general) meaning of the promise: "Jesus answered, 'You do not know now what I am doing [that is, foot washing], but later you will understand.'" The coffee remains unbought, but readers are invited to contend for it as well.

4. Thomas V. Morris, *Making Sense of It All: Pascal and the Meaning of Life* (Grand Rapids, MI: Eerdmans, 1992), 86.

5. A student of mine once sensibly inquired why God couldn't just expand human intelligence so that it *could* comprehend God's providence. This is a difficult question to answer, because it raises the issue of whether such a change in intelligence would produce a change in the *kind* of being we are, rather than simply a difference in *degree* of intelligence we possess. Would it continue to make sense to call us humans at that point? Would it matter? Such a query also begs the question of our *moral* maturity. Still, the next discussion is prepared to grant this possibility for sake of argument. And chapter 7 argues that, in fact, such a question is finally beside the point: lack of intelligence is not our main problem.

6. I thank Neal Plantinga for this vivid phrase.

7. Peter Kreeft puts this point nicely in Peter Kreeft, *Making Sense Out of Suffering* (Ann Arbor, MI: Servant Books, 1986), 23.

8. Sarah F. Bence, on a final examination written at the University of Manitoba in May 1997.

9. Some readers will correctly notice that I am directly contradicting Rabbi Harold Kushner's conclusions about Job in chapter 2 of his book, *When Bad Things Happen to Good People* (New York: Avon, 1981). For an alternative interpretation of Job, I recommend Philip Yancey, *Disappointment with God: Three Questions No One Asks Aloud* (Grand Rapids, MI: Zondervan, 1988), 161–255.

10. Blocher, *Evil and the Cross*, 54. Though I invoke Hick in this regard, it should be evident from the foregoing that I do not thereby endorse his

view that the Fall was virtually inevitable as the starting point for the program of human "soul-making." The Fall was a disaster, whatever blessing God has been able to yield out of it. See also Thomas Morris's exposition of Blaise Pascal's *Pensées* on this matter: "The Hidden God," in Morris, *Making Sense of It All*, 85–108.

11. Thus I am recommending a shift from theodicy to what some philosophers call "meta-theodicy," an explanation of why a theodicy is not available to us and what rational grounds can be advanced for believing in God in the face of evil anyway. (For a brief introduction to this issue, see Michael L. Peterson, "Introduction," in *The Problem of Evil: Selected Readings*, ed. Michael L. Peterson [Notre Dame, IN: University of Notre Dame Press, 1992], 8–10.) This approach responds technically to the so-called evidential or probabilistic argument against theism on the basis of evil, the argument that the presence of evil (and, in some forms of this argument, *this much* or even *gratuitous* evil) may not render theism logically inconsistent, but it does make it highly implausible. As several others have pointed out, however, any assessment of the relative probabilities of theism versus atheism must take into account far more than just the presence of evil in the world. For the atheist to win his point, he must show that the presence of evil in the world amounts to more telling evidence against the existence of an all-good and all-powerful God than all of the evidences for the existence of such a God. And no atheist (or any other critic of theism) has accomplished this feat. (William Rowe, himself a distinguished philosopher on this subject and a vigorous opponent of theism, agrees: see his discussion in William L. Rowe, *Philosophy of Religion: An Introduction*, 2nd ed. [Belmont, CA: Wadsworth, 1993], 79–89). In what follows, I intend to make the work of such a critic as challenging as I can.

12. C. S. Lewis muses that there must be powerful warrants for belief in God *somewhere* precisely because the problem of evil is so difficult: "If the universe is so bad, or even half so bad, how on earth did human beings ever come to attribute it to the activity of a wise and good Creator? Men are fools, perhaps; but hardly so foolish as that. The direct inference from black to white, from evil flower to virtuous root, from senseless work to a workman infinitely wise, staggers belief. The spectacle of the universe as revealed by experience can never have been the ground of [such] religion: it must always have been something *in spite of which*

[such] religion, acquired from a different source, was held" (*The Problem of Pain* [New York: Collier Macmillan, 1962], 15; emphasis added).

13. I am indebted to an essay of Brian Gerrish that first acquainted me with the thought of Luther and Calvin on the *deus absconditus* (the "hidden God"): B. A. Gerrish, "'To the Unknown God': Luther and Calvin on the Hiddenness of God," in *The Old Protestantism and the New: Essays on the Reformation Heritage* (Chicago: University of Chicago Press, 1982), 131–49.

14. For examples of such polling in North America, see George Gallup Jr. and Sarah Jones, *100 Questions and Answers: Religion in America* (Princeton, NJ: Princeton Religion Research Center, 1989); and Reginald W. Bibby, *Unknown Gods: The Ongoing Story of Religion in Canada* (Toronto: Stoddart, 1993).

15. Kreeft, *Making Sense Out of Suffering*, 95.

16. On Jewish expectations regarding Messiah, see N. T. Wright, *The New Testament and the People of God* (Minneapolis, MN: Fortress, 1992), 307–20.

17. An important recent work on this subject is Larry W. Hurtado, *One God, One Lord: Early Christian Devotion and Ancient Jewish Monotheism* (Philadelphia: Fortress, 1988).

18. Dorothy L. Sayers, "The Greatest Drama Ever Staged," in *The Whimsical Christian* (New York: Collier Macmillan, 1987), 12.

19. Standard treatments of these two images are, respectively, John R. W. Stott, *The Cross of Christ* (Downers Grove, IL: InterVarsity, 1986); and Gustav Aulén, *Christus Victor: A Historical Study of the Three Main Types of the Idea of the Atonement*, trans. A. G. Hebert (New York: Macmillan, 1969).

20. *The Brothers Karamazov*, 281.

21. And may I say as a father of three sons that God suffers also as God the Father who sends his own Son to the Cross and is pierced by the agony of letting that Child go through all of that torture—for the likes of us. Only in the mystery of the Trinity could the one God both suffer on the Cross and then suffer as Parent grieving over Child.

22. Three recent inquiries into Jesus' resurrection deserve note here: William Lane Craig, *Assessing the New Testament Evidence for the Historicity of the Resurrection of Jesus*, Studies in the Bible and Early Christianity 16 (Lewiston, NY: Edwin Mellen, 1989); Stephen T. Davis, *Risen Indeed: Making Sense of the Resurrection* (Grand Rapids, MI: Eerdmans, 1993); and C. Stephen Evans, *The Historical Christ and the Jesus of Faith: The Incarnational Narrative as History* (Oxford: Clarendon Press, 1996). For alternative views, see Gavin D'Costa, ed., *Resurrection Reconsidered* (Oxford: Oneworld, 1996).

23. Yancey, *Disappointment*, 150.
24. Dorothy L. Sayers, "The Faust Legend and the Idea of the Devil," in *The Whimsical Christian*, 262.
25. *Problem of Pain*, 128.
26. C. Stephen Layman, "Faith Has Its Reasons," in *God and the Philosophers: The Reconciliation of Faith and Reason*, ed. Thomas V. Morris (New York: Oxford University Press, 1994), 90.
27. I am mindful of James Wetzel's criticism of theodicy that "it cannot accept the possibility of irredeemable evil." I think theodicy in fact must do so, and hell is the most powerful symbol Christian thought has for this terrible acceptance (James Wetzel, "Can Theodicy Be Avoided? The Claim of Unredeemed Evil," *Religious Studies* 25 [1989]; reprinted in Peterson, ed., *The Problem of Evil*, 359; cf. p. 365 n. 18).
28. L. Stafford Betty, "Making Sense of Animal Pain: An Environmental Theodicy," *Faith and Philosophy* 9 (January 1992):69. I thank Scott Dunbar for drawing this article to my attention.
29. Yancey, *Disappointment*, 244.
30. C. S. Lewis, *The Weight of Glory and Other Essays* (Grand Rapids, MI: Eerdmans, 1979 [1949]), 1–2.
31. I thank Marie Loewen for reminding me of this in her comments on an earlier draft of this book.
32. Again, I thank Marie Loewen for this observation.
33. No less an authority than Bruce M. Metzger, Professor Emeritus of New Testament at Princeton Theological Seminary and chairman of the New Revised Standard Version translation committee, recently commented with evident exasperation: "No other field of ancient history has seen such a mushrooming of guesswork as copious as this. With so many images of Jesus being produced, one would expect some embarrassment over a supposedly rational method that yields such widely divergent results" (review of Luke Timothy Johnson's *The Real Jesus: The Misguided Quest for the Historical Jesus and the Truth of the Traditional Gospels*, in *Religious and Theological Students Fellowship Bulletin* 11 [March/April 1996]:16).
34. Standard works on the history of modern New Testament scholarship are the following: Werner Georg Kümmel, *The New Testament: The History of the Investigation of Its Problems*, trans. S. MacLean Gilmour and Howard Clark Kee (Nashville, TN, and New York: Abingdon, 1972 [1970]); and Stephen Neill and Tom Wright, *The Interpretation of the New Testament*,

1861–1986 (New York: Oxford University Press, 1988). For provocative exchanges regarding the state of the art, see Eleonore Stump and Thomas P. Flint, eds., *Hermes and Athena: Biblical Exegesis and Philosophical Theology* (Notre Dame, IN: University of Notre Dame Press, 1993).

35. On the question of the historicity of the gospels, see Paul Barnett, *Is the New Testament Reliable?: A Look at the Historical Evidence* (Downers Grove, IL: InterVarsity Press, 1986); and Craig Blomberg, *The Historical Reliability of the Gospels* (Downers Grove, IL: InterVarsity Press, 1987). On the question of how the early church came to recognize these four Gospels and not others as authoritative, see two recent accounts: F. F. Bruce, *The Canon of Scripture* (Downers Grove, IL: InterVarsity Press, 1988); and Harry Y. Gamble, "Canon: New Testament," in *The Anchor Bible Dictionary*, ed. David Noel Freedman et al. (New York: Doubleday, 1992), 1:852–61.

36. Morris, *Making Sense of It All*, 175.

37. Ibid., 174.

38. Chesterton, *Orthodoxy* (Garden City, NY: Image/Doubleday, 1959 [1908]), 83.

39. For critical testimonies to this effect, see Kelly James Clark, ed., *Philosophers Who Believe: The Spiritual Journeys of 11 Leading Thinkers* (Downers Grove, IL: InterVarsity Press, 1993); and Thomas V. Morris, ed., *God and the Philosophers: The Reconciliation of Faith and Reason* (New York: Oxford University Press, 1994). For a presentation of the Christian worldview, see Arthur F. Holmes, *Contours of a World View* (Grand Rapids, MI: Eerdmans, 1984 [1983]).

40. Kreeft, *Making Sense Out of Suffering*, 4.

Chapter Seven   *Thinking and Living*

1. For a technical introduction to the state of the art, see Alvin Plantinga, *Warrant: The Current Debate* (New York and Oxford: Oxford University Press, 1993).

2. Linda Trinkaus Zagzebski, "Vocatio Philosophiae," in *Philosophers Who Believe: The Spiritual Journeys of 11 Leading Thinkers*, ed. Kelly James Clark (Downers Grove, IL: InterVarsity Press, 1993), 239.

3. Philip Yancey, *Disappointment with God: Three Questions No One Asks Aloud* (Grand Rapids, MI: Zondervan, 1988), 43–49.

4. John Hick writes that "perhaps there *are* challenges and tasks, problems and pains in heaven. For the Christian conception of heaven is not basi-

cally that of a pain-free paradise, but that of life lived in a wholly right relationship to God. There could not be unhappiness within such a relationship; but there might (for all that we can now know) be difficult tasks, not to be performed without the endurance of even great hardship and pain, and immense and challenging problems, to be solved only by intense effort" (*Evil and the God of Love*, 2nd. ed. [London: Macmillan, 1977], 351–52).

5. Thomas V. Morris, *Making Sense of It All: Pascal and the Meaning of Life* (Grand Rapids, MI: Eerdmans, 1992), 15.

6. These questions are raised in Hugh Silvester, *Arguing with God* (Downers Grove, IL: InterVarsity Press, 1971).

7. Henri Blocher, *Evil and the Cross*, trans. David G. Preston (Downers Grove, IL: InterVarsity Press, 1994 [1990]), 103.

8. Marilyn McCord Adams, "Redemptive Suffering: A Christian Solution to the Problem of Evil," in *Rationality, Religious Belief and Moral Commitment*, ed. Robert Audi and William J. Wainwright (Ithaca, NY: Cornell University Press, 1986); reprinted in *The Problem of Evil: Selected Readings*, ed. Michael L. Peterson (Notre Dame, IN: University of Notre Dame Press, 1992), 179.

INDEX

Index

Index